Teach & Test

Language Grade 4

Table of Contents

How to Use This Book

1. This book can be used in a home or classroom setting. Read through each unit before working with the student(s). Familiarize yourself with the vocabulary and the skills that are introduced at the top of each unit activity page. Use this information as a guide to help instruct the student(s).

2. Choose a quiet place with little or no interruptions (including the telephone). Talk with the student(s) about the purpose of this book and how you will be working as a team to prepare for standardized tests.

3. As an option, copy the unit test and give it as a pretest to identify weak areas.

4. Upon the completion of each unit, you will find a unit test. Discuss the Helping Hand strategy for test taking featured on the test. Use the example on each test as a chance to show the student(s) how to work through a problem and completely fill in the answer circle. Encourage the student(s) to work independently when possible, but this is a learning time, and questions should be welcomed. A time limit is given for each test. Instruct the student(s) to use the time allowed efficiently, looking back over the answers if possible. Tell him to continue until he sees the stop sign.

5. Record the score on the record sheet on page 4. If a student has difficulty with any questions, use the cross-reference guide on the inside back cover to identify the skills that need to be reviewed.

Teach & Test
Introduction

Now this makes sense—teaching students the skills and strategies that are expected of them before they are tested!

Many students, parents, and teachers are concerned that standardized test scores do not adequately reflect a child's capabilities. This may be due to one or more of the factors italicized below. The purpose of this book is to reduce the negative impact of these, or similar factors, on a student's standardized test scores. The goal is to target those factors and alter their effects as described.

1. *The student has been taught the tested skills but has forgotten them.* This book is divided into units that are organized similarly to fourth grade textbooks. Instructions for the skill itself are found at the top of each unit activity page, ensuring that the student has been exposed to each key component. The exercises include drill/practice and creative learning activities. Additional activity suggestions can be found in a star burst within the units. These activities require the students to apply the skills that they are practicing.

2. *The student has mastered the skills but has never seen them presented in a test-type format.* Ideally, the skills a student learns at school will be used as part of problem solving in the outside world. For this reason, the skills in this book, and in most classrooms, are not practiced in a test-type format. At the end of each unit in this book, the skills are specifically matched with test questions. In this way, the book serves as a type of "bridge" between the skills that the student(s) has mastered and the standardized test format.

3. *The student is inexperienced with the answer sheet format.* Depending on the standardized test that your school district uses, students are expected to fill in the answer circles completely and neatly. The unit, midway review, and final review tests will help prepare the student(s) for this process.

4. *The student may feel the anxiety of a new and unfamiliar situation.* While testing, students will notice changes in their daily routine: their classroom door will be closed with a "Testing" sign on it, they will be asked not to use the restroom, their desks may be separated, their teacher may read from a script and refuse to repeat herself, etc. To help relieve the stress caused by these changes, treat each unit test in this book as it would be treated at school by following the procedures listed below.

Stage a Test

You will find review tests midway through the book and again at the end of the book. When you reach these points, "stage a test" by creating a real test-taking environment. The procedures listed below coincide with many standardized test directions. The purpose is to alleviate stress, rather than contribute to it, so make this a serious, but calm, event and the student(s) will benefit.

1. Prepare! Have the student(s) sharpen two pencils, lay out scratch paper, and use the restroom.

2. Choose a room with a door that can be closed. Ask a student to put a sign on the door that reads "Testing" and explain that no talking will be permitted after the sign is hung.

3. Direct the student(s) to turn to a specific page but not to begin until the instructions are completely given.

4. Read the instructions at the top of the page and work through the example together. Discuss the Helping Hand strategy that is featured at the top of the page. Have the student(s) neatly and completely fill in the bubble for the example. This is the child's last chance to ask for help!

5. Instruct the student(s) to continue working until the stop sign is reached. If a student needs help reading, you may read each question only once.

Helping Hand Test Strategies

The first page of each test features a specific test-taking strategy that will be helpful in working through most standardized tests. These strategies are introduced and spotlighted one at a time so that they will be learned and remembered internally. Each will serve as a valuable test-taking tool, so discuss them thoroughly.

The strategies include:

- Sometimes the correct answer is not given. Fill in the circle beside NG if no answer is correct.
- Always read each question carefully.
- Read all the answer choices before you choose the one you think is correct.
- Fill in the answer circles completely and neatly.
- Cross out answers you know are wrong.
- Use your time wisely. If a question seems too tough, skip it and come back to it later.
- Take time to review your answers.

Constructed-Response Questions

You will find the final question of each test is written in a different format called constructed response. This means that students are not provided with answer choices, but are instead asked to construct their own answers. The objective of such an "open-ended" type of question is to provide students with a chance to creatively develop reasonable answers. It also provides an insight to a student's reasoning and thinking skills. As this format is becoming more accepted and encouraged by standardized test developers, students will be "ahead of the game" by practicing such responses now.

Evaluating the Tests

Two types of questions are included in each test. The unit tests and the midway review test each consist of 20 multiple-choice questions, and the final review test consists of 30 multiple-choice questions. All tests include a constructed-response question which requires the student(s) to construct and sometimes support an answer. Use the following procedures to evaluate a student's performance on each test.

1. Use the answer key found on pages 125–128 to correct the tests. Be sure the student(s) neatly and completely filled in the answer circles.

2. Record the scores on the record sheet found on page 4. If the student(s) incorrectly answered any questions, use the cross-reference guide found on the inside back cover to help identify the skills the student(s) needs to review. Each test question references the corresponding activity page.

3. Scoring the constructed-response questions is somewhat subjective. Discuss these questions with the student(s). Sometimes it is easier for the student(s) to explain the answer verbally. Help the student to record her thoughts as a written answer. If the student(s) has difficulty formulating a response, refer back to the activity pages using the cross-reference guide. Also review the star burst activity found in the unit which also requires the student(s) to formulate an answer.

4. Discuss the test with the student(s). What strategies were used to answer the questions? Were some questions more difficult than others? Was there enough time? What strategies did the student(s) use while taking the test?

Record Sheet

Record a student's score for each test by drawing a star or placing a sticker below each item number that was correct. Leave the incorrect boxes empty as this will allow you to visually see any weak spots. Review and practice those missed skills, then retest only the necessary items.

Unit 1

1	2	3	4	5	6	7	8	9	10	11	12	13	14	15	16	17	18	19	20

Unit 2

1	2	3	4	5	6	7	8	9	10	11	12	13	14	15	16	17	18	19	20

Unit 3

1	2	3	4	5	6	7	8	9	10	11	12	13	14	15	16	17	18	19	20

Unit 4

1	2	3	4	5	6	7	8	9	10	11	12	13	14	15	16	17	18	19	20

Midway Review Test

1	2	3	4	5	6	7	8	9	10	11	12	13	14	15	16	17	18	19	20

Unit 5

1	2	3	4	5	6	7	8	9	10	11	12	13	14	15	16	17	18	19	20

Unit 6

1	2	3	4	5	6	7	8	9	10	11	12	13	14	15	16	17	18	19	20

Unit 7

1	2	3	4	5	6	7	8	9	10	11	12	13	14	15	16	17	18	19	20

Final Review Test

1	2	3	4	5	6	7	8	9	10	11	12	13	14	15	16	17	18	19	20

21	22	23	24	25	26	27	28	29	30

Name

Common nouns
A **common noun** names a person, place, or thing.
Examples: <u>cowhand</u> (person), <u>ranch</u> (place), <u>herd</u> (thing)

Name That Noun

Write each common noun from the Word Bank under the correct heading.

valley	athlete	canyon	acrobat	mountain
buffalo	hilltop	jungle	pasture	feast
courtyard	diver	raccoon	manager	moment
senator	fountain	owner	wedding	directors

People	**Places**	**Things**
_____	_____	_____
_____	_____	_____
_____	_____	_____
_____	_____	_____
_____	_____	_____
_____	_____	_____

Write four sentences with a common noun for a person, a place, and a thing in each one. Use your own words or choose some from the lists you made above. Underline each common noun you use in the sentences.

Example: The <u>cowhand</u> on the <u>ranch</u> watched the <u>herd</u>.

1. _____

2. _____

3. _____

4. _____

Name

Proper nouns

A **proper noun** names a special person, place, or thing. A proper noun begins with a capital letter.

Examples: <u>Abraham Lincoln</u> was the sixteenth president. (special person) He lived in the <u>White House</u>. (special place) He was president during the <u>Civil War</u>. (special thing)

America's Home

Underline each proper noun in the sentences below.

1. The official home of the president of the United States is at 1600 Pennsylvania Avenue.

2. George Washington did not live in the President's House.

3. John Adams and his wife, Abigail, were the first to live there.

4. The British burned the President's House during the War of 1812, so President Monroe lived near 20th Street for nine months.

5. Andrew Jackson had magnolia trees planted on the south lawn called President's Park.

6. President Roosevelt changed the name to the White House in 1901.

7. Another name for the White House is the Executive Mansion.

8. The children of Theodore Roosevelt and their friends became known as "The White House Gang."

9. President Johnson gave a speech in the Rose Garden.

10. President George Bush was president during the Gulf War in 1991.

11. President Clinton had a dog named Buddy.

12. Barbara and Jenna are the twin daughters of President George W. Bush.

Name

Identifying singular and plural nouns

A **singular noun** names one person, place, or thing. Examples: violinist, stage, violin

A **plural noun** names more than one person, place, or thing. It often ends in **-s** or **-es**.
Examples: violinists, stages, violins

One or More Than One?

Write **S** for singular if the common noun names one person. Write **P** for plural if it names more than one person.

_____ 1. woman   _____ 2. strangers   _____ 3. lady

_____ 4. fellows   _____ 5. guest   _____ 6. toddler

_____ 7. teammates   _____ 8. widows   _____ 9. enemies

_____ 10. neighbor   _____ 11. partner   _____ 12. pioneers

Write **S** for singular if the common noun names one place. Write **P** for plural if it names more than one place.

_____ 13. skyscraper   _____ 14. gym   _____ 15. airports

_____ 16. factories   _____ 17. restaurant   _____ 18. temple

_____ 19. hospital   _____ 20. motels   _____ 21. malls

_____ 22. beaches   _____ 23. capitol   _____ 24. cottages

Write **S** for singular if the common noun names one thing.
Write **P** for plural if it names more than one thing.

_____ 25. sailboats   _____ 26. parachutes

_____ 27. ramp   _____ 28. freeways

_____ 29. legend   _____ 30. journals

_____ 31. bulldozers   _____ 32. subway

_____ 33. headlights   _____ 34. telegrams

_____ 35. wishes   _____ 36. bicycles

Name

Making nouns plural   Unit 1

A **plural noun** names more than one person, place, or thing. Add **-s** to most singular nouns to make them plural. Example: book<u>s</u>

If a singular noun ends with **sh, ch, x, s,** or **z,** add **-es** to make it plural. Example: beach<u>es</u>

Plenty of Plurals

Write the plural of each singular noun by adding **-s** or **-es**.

1. wagon _____

2. glass _____

3. niece _____

4. trench _____

5. branch _____

6. myth _____

7. dress _____

8. marsh _____

9. glacier _____

10. zipper _____

11. speech _____

12. invitation _____

13. wish _____

14. sleigh _____

15. mask _____

16. tax _____

17. buzz _____

18. brush _____

19. wrinkle _____

20. patch _____

Complete each sentence with the plural of the noun in parentheses.

21. Kangaroos are furry _____ that live in Australia. (mammal)

22. Red kangaroos live in the _____ and grasslands. (desert)

23. Gray kangaroos inhabit the _____ and grasslands. (forest)

24. Female kangaroos have pocket-like _____. (pouch)

25. Kangaroos have long hind _____ and feet. (leg)

Name _____

A **plural noun** names more than one person, place, or thing. If a singular noun ends with a consonant followed by **-y**, change the **-y** to **-i**, and add **-es** to make the word plural.
Example: baby/bab<u>ies</u>

If the singular noun ends with a vowel followed by **-y**, just add **-s** to make the plural.
Example: boy/boy<u>s</u>

Practical Plurals

Write the plural of each singular noun.

1. bunny _____
2. daisy _____
3. lady _____
4. navy _____
5. city _____
6. turkey _____
7. hobby _____
8. casualty _____
9. puppy _____
10. mummy _____
11. copy _____
12. library _____

Some nouns have irregular plural forms. Draw a line to match each singular noun to its irregular plural form.

Singular	Plural	Singular	Plural
13. man	feet	14. child	mice
15. deer	deer	16. goose	women
17. foot	oxen	18. mouse	children
19. ox	men	20. woman	geese

Write the sentence using the plural form of each underlined noun.

21. The <u>man</u> chased the <u>ox</u> down the road.

_____

22. The <u>woman</u> and the <u>child</u> fed the <u>goose</u>.

_____

Name _____

A **possessive noun** is a word that shows who or what has something or owns something. Add an apostrophe and **-s** (**'s**) to most singular common and proper nouns to show possession. Examples: girl/girl's, Sue/Sue's

Add an apostrophe (') to most plural common and proper nouns to show possession. Examples: cars/cars', Taylors/Taylors'

Add an apostrophe and **-s** (**'s**) to irregular plural nouns to show possession. Example: teeth/teeth's

Possessive Power

Write the possessive form of each noun.

1. tooth _____

2. Pacific _____

3. Yankees _____

4. players _____

5. men _____

6. reptiles _____

7. berries _____

8. course _____

9. plant _____

10. flowers _____

11. women _____

12. Paula _____

Rewrite each phrase below using a possessive noun for each underlined noun. Follow the example.

Example: the coat belonging to the boy/ the boy's coat

13. the dances of the ballerinas _____

14. the delicious taste of the cookies _____

15. the meeting of the women _____

16. the playground of the children _____

17. the win of the Mets _____

18. the fluffy tail of the rabbit _____

19. the pencils of the pupils _____

Name _____

Subject pronouns

You and **I** are pronouns that can be used as the subject of a sentence. They can stand alone. Example: <u>You</u> and <u>I</u> enjoy watching bicycle races.

He, she, it, we, and **they** are **subject pronouns** that can replace nouns and phrases containing nouns in the subject part of a sentence. Example: <u>The Tour de France</u> is a bicycle race. <u>It</u> is a bicycle race.

Off to the Races!

Write **he, she, it, we,** or **they** to replace each word or group of words below.

1. mountain _____   2. audience _____

3. Greg _____   4. you and I _____

5. bicycles _____   6. mother _____

7. racers _____   8. Lance _____

Rewrite each sentence substituting a subject pronoun for the underlined word or words.

9. <u>Bicycle racing</u> is popular all over the world.

_____

10. <u>Racers from different countries</u> compete in road races.

_____

11. <u>The Tour de France</u> lasts three weeks and covers about 2,400 miles.

_____

12. <u>Mom</u> told me that Greg LeMond won that race three times!

_____

13. <u>You and I</u> read about another great American road racer.

_____

14. <u>Lance Armstrong</u> won the Tour de France in 1999, 2000, and 2001.

_____

Name _____

Object pronouns

An **object pronoun** is used in the predicate of a sentence. They receive the action of the verb. **You** and **me** are object pronouns that can stand alone.
Example: Mr. Wilson told <u>you</u> and <u>me</u> about recycling materials.

Him, her, it, us, and **them** are object pronouns. Example: Recycling materials helps <u>the environment</u>. Recycling materials helps <u>it</u>.

Reuse, Reduce, Recycle

Write **him**, **her**, **it**, **us**, or **them** to replace each word or group of words below.

1. trash _____

2. pollution _____

3. Mr. Wilson _____

4. newspapers _____

5. aluminum _____

6. landfills _____

7. you and me _____

8. Carol _____

Rewrite each sentence substituting an object pronoun for the underlined word or words.

9. Mr. Wilson told <u>our class</u> about recycling materials.

_____

10. Recycling reuses <u>waste materials</u>.

_____

11. Waste materials include <u>aluminum and steel cans</u>.

_____

12. Carol asked <u>Mr. Wilson</u> if glass containers can be reused.

_____

13. He told <u>Carol</u> that glass and plastics are recyclable.

_____

14. Recycling reduces <u>pollution</u> from waste materials.

_____

Subject and object pronouns   Unit 1

You and **I** are pronouns that can be used as the subject of a sentence. They can stand alone. Examples: I like to study American history. You know a lot about the pioneers.

He, she, it, we, and **they** are **subject pronouns** that can replace nouns and phrases containing nouns in the subject of a sentence. Example: Pioneers crossed the mountains. They followed Indian trails. (*They* refers to *pioneers*.)

An **object pronoun** is used in the predicate of a sentence. It receives the action of the verb. **You** and **me** are object pronouns that can stand alone. Example: Dad tells you and me about the early pioneers. (*Tells* is the verb.)

Him, her, it, us, and **them** are object pronouns that can replace nouns and noun phrases in the predicate of a sentence. Example: Pioneers crossed the mountains. Pioneers crossed them. (*Them* refers to the *mountains*.)

Westward, Ho!

Rewrite each sentence substituting the correct pronoun for the underlined word or words.

1. Some pioneers traveled west in boats.

   _____

2. The Erie Canal was an important waterway.

   _____

3. Daniel Boone and his men cut the Wilderness Road in 1775.

   _____

4. The road made travel through the Cumberland Gap easier.

   _____

5. My great-grandparents joined other pioneers on the long trip west.

   _____

6. My great-grandfather took an ax, a rifle, and a few tools for farming.

   _____

7. He probably took a hoe to plant the first crop.

   _____

Name

Possessive pronouns

My, your, her, his, its, our, and **their** are **possessive pronouns** that show who or what has something or owns something. Use these possessive pronouns in front of nouns. Example: <u>My</u> report is about an unusual African animal.

Mine, yours, his, hers, ours, and **theirs** are **possessive pronouns** that can stand alone. Example: <u>Mine</u> is about aardvarks.

Amazing Aardvarks

Rewrite each sentence substituting the correct possessive pronoun for the underlined word or words.

1. <u>The aardvarks'</u> appearance may look strange to us.

   _____

2. <u>Aardvarks'</u> bodies are arched, and they have long snouts.

   _____

3. An aardvark's ears are large, and <u>an aardvark's</u> tail is long.

   _____

4. <u>An aardvark's</u> diet consists of ants and termites.

   _____

5. <u>A female aardvark's</u> baby is born at the beginning of the rainy season.

   _____

6. A male baby stays with <u>a male baby's</u> mother for about a year.

   _____

7. <u>My next science report</u> will be on anteaters.

   _____

8. What will <u>your report</u> be about?

   _____

Name

Read or listen to the directions. Fill in the circle beside the best answer.

☐ Example:

Which word is not a common noun?

(A) uncle

(B) James

(C) airport

(D) luggage

Answer: B because it names a special person and begins with a capital letter.

Sometimes the correct answer is not given. Fill in the circle beside NG if no answer is correct.

Now try these. You have 20 minutes. Continue until you see STOP .

What is the common noun in the sentence?

1. Christopher practices his clarinet.

Christopher	practices	his	clarinet
(A)	(B)	(C)	(D)

2. He plays in the orchestra.

He	plays	in	orchestra
(A)	(B)	(C)	(D)

3. Which is the proper noun that names a person in the sentence?

George Washington grew up in Virginia and was the first president of the United States of America.

(A) George Washington

(B) Virginia

(C) United States

(D) America

GO ON

Name

4. Which is a proper noun that names a place?

George Washington lived at Mount Vernon as a youth.

(A) George Washington   (B) lived

(C) Mount Vernon   (D) youth

5. Which is a proper noun that names a thing?

George Washington helped write the Constitution in Philadelphia.

(A) George Washington   (B) helped

(C) Constitution   (D) Philadelphia

Which of the underlined words is not a proper noun?

6. <u>Robert Peary</u> and <u>Matthew Henson</u> and four other <u>men</u> reached the <u>North Pole</u> in 1909.

| Robert Peary | men | Matthew Henson | North Pole |
| (A) | (B) | (C) | (D) |

7. <u>Naomi Uemura</u> of <u>Japan</u> was the first <u>person</u> to reach the <u>North Pole</u> alone.

| Naomi Uemura | Japan | person | North Pole |
| (A) | (B) | (C) | (D) |

Which word is a singular noun?

8.

| factories | workers | machine | products |
| (A) | (B) | (C) | (D) |

9.

| doctors | hospital | nurses | patients |
| (A) | (B) | (C) | (D) |

GO ON

Unit 1 Test

Which word is not a plural noun?

10.   headline   reporters   newspapers   presses
             Ⓐ   Ⓑ   Ⓒ   Ⓓ

11.   oceans   whale   scientists   studies
             Ⓐ   Ⓑ   Ⓒ   Ⓓ

Choose the correct plural form of the noun.

12. branch   branchs   branchies   branches   branched
             Ⓐ   Ⓑ   Ⓒ   Ⓓ

13. mouse   mouses   mice   mices   mousy
             Ⓐ   Ⓑ   Ⓒ   Ⓓ

Choose the correct possessive form of the noun.

14. children   child's   childrens   children's   NG
             Ⓐ   Ⓑ   Ⓒ   Ⓓ

15. baby   babies   babys'   babies'   baby's
             Ⓐ   Ⓑ   Ⓒ   Ⓓ

Choose the correct pronoun for the underlined word or words.

16. <u>My uncle</u> is a volcanologist.

     She   He   They   It
     Ⓐ   Ⓑ   Ⓒ   Ⓓ

Choose the correct pronoun for the underlined word or words.

17. Uncle Leo studies <u>volcanoes</u>.

they	it	him	them
Ⓐ	Ⓑ	Ⓒ	Ⓓ

18. <u>Uncle Leo's</u> research has taken him all over the world.

Its	His	He	Their
Ⓐ	Ⓑ	Ⓒ	Ⓓ

Which word in the sentence is a possessive pronoun?

19. Yours is the most beautiful castle that he and I have seen.

most	he	I	NG
Ⓐ	Ⓑ	Ⓒ	Ⓓ

20. We saw its magnificent view when we visited you.

We	its	you	NG
Ⓐ	Ⓑ	Ⓒ	Ⓓ

Write a sentence with a subject pronoun. Rewrite the sentence using a proper noun for the subject pronoun.

_____

_____

_____

Present tense action verbs   Unit 2

A **present tense action verb** shows action that is happening now. Present tense action verbs end in **-s** or **-es** when the noun in the subject part of a sentence is singular. Examples: The <u>boy</u> stretches. The <u>boys</u> stretch.

Water, Water, Everywhere

Is the word an action verb? Circle yes or no for the correct answer.

1. vocal   yes   no   2. suddenly   yes   no

3. annoys   yes   no   4. vote   yes   no

5. paddle   yes   no   6. catches   yes   no

7. recopy   yes   no   8. gobble   yes   no

9. connects   yes   no   10. intelligent yes   no

11. breathe   yes   no   12. teases   yes   no

13. energy   yes   no   14. approach   yes   no

15. compare   yes   no   16. creature   yes   no

Underline the action verb in each sentence.

17. People need clean, fresh drinking water.

18. Farmers use water to irrigate their fields.

19. Power plants produce electricity using water.

20. Lakes and rivers provide recreation areas for people.

21. Population growth causes increased demand for water.

22. Expanding industry and agriculture require more water.

23. Some parts of the world face water shortages.

24. People drill for water in some areas.

25. People also dam rivers to make reservoirs.

26. Other areas of the world receive too much water.

Name

Present tense action verbs and linking verbs

A **present tense action verb** shows action that is happening now. Present tense action verbs end in **-s** or **-es** when the noun in the subject is singular. Example: It <u>jumps</u>.

A **linking verb** does not show action. It links the subject of a sentence to a noun or adjective in the predicate. Present tense forms of the verb **be**—*am, is, are*—and the verb **have**—*have, has*—are common linking verbs. *Seem, appear,* and *become* are also linking verbs. Example: It <u>is</u> funny.

Mexican Jumping Beans

Identify each word as an **action** verb, a **linking** verb, or **neither**.

1. bury _____

2. concrete _____

3. hatch _____

4. seems _____

5. legal _____

6. investigate _____

7. study _____

8. pretend _____

9. becomes _____

10. am _____

Write the correct present tense form of each action verb or linking verb in parentheses to complete each sentence.

11. The jumping bean _____ a seed of a Mexican bush. (is, are)

12. A person can actually _____ the seed jump. (see, sees)

13. First, a moth _____ its eggs on the bush's flowers. (lay, lays)

14. The eggs _____, and caterpillars emerge. (hatch, hatches)

15. Then the caterpillars _____ into the bush's seeds. (burrow, burrows)

16. The caterpillar _____ the inside of the seed, leaving the outer shell. (eat, eats)

17. It _____ a web inside the hollow seed. (build, builds)

18. The insect _____ the web and jerks its body. (grab, grabs)

19. The seed _____ ! (jump, jumps)

20. The jumping bean _____ active for several months. (appear, appears)

Name _____

Past tense action verbs

A **past tense action verb** shows action that has already happened. The past tense of most action verbs is made by adding **-ed** to the present tense verb. Example: talk/talk**ed**

However, if the verb ends in a silent **-e**, drop the **-e** and add **-ed**. Example: like/lik**ed**

If the verb ends with a single consonant preceded by a single vowel, double the consonant and add **-ed**. Example: grab/grab**bed**

If the verb ends in a consonant and **-y**, change the **-y** to **-i** and add **-ed** to write the past tense. Example: carry/carr**ied**

Tammy Tadpole

Write the past tense of each present tense action verb.

1. explain _____   2. hug _____

3. fan _____   4. twist _____

5. marry _____   6. study _____

7. destroy _____   8. deny _____

Write the past tense of the present tense verb in parentheses to complete each sentence.

9. Tammy Tadpole _____ from an egg in a pond. (hatch)

10. Tammy _____ in a shallow pond in the woods. (live)

11. She _____ like a small fish at first. (look)

12. The tadpole _____ her tail to swim. (use)

13. She _____ with gills. (breathe)

14. Her appearance _____ after a few weeks. (change)

15. She _____ to grow hind legs. (start)

16. Her head _____, and her tail shortened. (flatten)

17. Tammy's front legs _____ next. (appear)

18. Her gills _____, and she could breathe air through her lungs. (vanish)

Name

Past tense action verbs and linking verbs

A **past tense action verb** shows action that has already happened.
Example: I <u>learned</u> about George Washington Carver yesterday.

Linking verbs do not show action. They link the subject of a sentence to a noun or adjective in the predicate part. The past tense forms of the linking verb **be** are *was* and *were*. The past tense of the linking verb **have** is *had*. The past tense of the linking verb **become** is *became*. Example: His research <u>was</u> important. (*Was* links the noun in the subject to the adjective in the predicate.)

George Washington Carver

Underline each past tense action verb and linking verb. Then write **A** for action or **L** for linking.

_____ 1. George Washington Carver was an American scientist.

_____ 2. He became famous for his agricultural research.

_____ 3. Carver discovered more than 300 products from peanuts.

_____ 4. He created more than 75 products from pecans.

_____ 5. He developed more than 100 products from sweet potatoes.

_____ 6. Carver encouraged southern farmers to try growing new crops.

_____ 7. He taught farmers about soil conservation.

_____ 8. Carver was head of Tuskegee Institute's Department of Research.

_____ 9. He received many awards for his contributions to science.

 Write one sentence for each of the following past tense linking verbs: was, were, had, became. Then underline the linking verb in each sentence. Circle the noun in the subject and the noun or adjective in the predicate that is linked by the verb.

Example: (Carver) <u>was</u> a (scientist.)

10. _____

11. _____

12. _____

13. _____

Name _____

Most past tense verbs are formed by adding **-ed** to the present tense forms.
Irregular verbs do not follow this rule.

Example of an irregular verb: **Present Tense**   **Past Tense**
                                   I <u>go</u> today.   I <u>went</u> yesterday.

'Gator Tales

Write the past tense of each irregular verb. If necessary, look up the present tense verb in the dictionary to learn the past tense.

1. wear _____   2. send _____

3. grow _____   4. catch _____

5. forgive _____   6. tell _____

7. speak _____   8. know _____

9. take _____   10. lose _____

11. steal _____   12. win _____

Rewrite each sentence. Use the past tense form of each underlined present tense irregular verb.

13. An alligator's eyes <u>stick</u> up on the top of its head.

_____

14. It <u>swims</u> by swishing its tail.

_____

15. A female alligator <u>sits</u> beside her nest.

_____

16. She <u>stands</u> near the nest to guard her eggs.

_____

17. The hatchlings <u>give</u> a high-pitched yelp.

_____

Name

Identifying helping verbs and main verbs

A **helping verb** is a word that is used with the main verb in the predicate part of a sentence. It helps tell about an action in the present, past, or future.

Forms of **be**—*am, is, are*—are helping verbs that tell about the present. Add **-ing** to the main verb. Examples: I <u>am</u> <u>studying</u> today. He <u>is</u> <u>studying</u>. We <u>are</u> <u>studying</u>.

Use *was* and *were* as helping verbs to tell about the past. Add **-ing** to the main verb. Examples: I <u>was</u> <u>studying</u> yesterday. We <u>were</u> <u>studying</u>.

Use *have* and *has* as helping verbs to tell about the past. Examples: I <u>have</u> <u>studied</u> before. She <u>has</u> <u>studied</u>.

Will and *shall* are helping verbs that are used to tell about the future. Examples: I <u>shall</u> <u>study</u> tomorrow. We <u>will</u> <u>study</u> together later.

Earth Day, Every Day

Underline the helping verb and circle the main verb in each sentence.

1. Rain forests have provided homes for millions of people.

2. Pygmies of central Africa have lived in rain forests for centuries.

3. Today, these people are making their livings by hunting, fishing, and farming.

4. Destruction of the rain forests is killing thousands of plants and animals each year.

5. Conservationists are working to preserve the rain forests.

6. Some governments had made laws in the past to protect different species.

7. More education is needed to make people aware of rain forests.

8. We will work together to protect the earth's rain forests.

Write **past, present,** or **future** to identify the tense of the underlined helping and main verbs.

9. Our school <u>has celebrated</u> Earth Day for over 20 years. _____

10. The students <u>have planted</u> trees on the school grounds every year. _____

11. This year my class <u>is planning</u> something different. _____

12. We <u>will make</u> posters to tell people about saving the rain forests. _____

13. Then we <u>shall put</u> them in restaurants and businesses all over town. _____

Name _____

Most past tense verbs used with the helping verbs *has* and *have* are formed by adding **-ed** to the present tense verb. **Irregular verbs** do not follow this rule. Examples: I <u>see</u> him. (present) I <u>saw</u> him. (past) I <u>have seen</u> him before. (past with a helping verb)

The Eyes Have It!

Fill in the chart with the correct forms of each irregular verb. Refer to a dictionary if needed.

Present	**Past**	**Past With Has or Have**
1. sing	_____	has or have sung
2. tell	told	has or have _____
3. _____	brought	has or have brought
4. wear	wore	has or have _____
5. take	_____	has or have taken
6. _____	stood	has or have stood

Write the past tense form of each irregular verb in parentheses.

7. Our teacher has _____ our class a book about insects. (read)

8. I had _____ that most insects have two compound eyes. (know)

9. Ms. Kemp _____ us that each eye has tiny six-sided lenses. (tell)

10. She has _____ before that some dragonflies have about 30,000 lenses. (say)

11. I had _____ that insects have no eyelids. (hear)

12. Scientists have _____ that insects cannot move or focus their eyes. (show)

13. We had _____, however, that insects can see movements. (understand)

14. Ms. Kemp has _____ science class interesting for us. (make)

Name _____

Contractions

A **contraction** is made by joining two words to make one new word. One or more letters are left out. An **apostrophe** (') is used in place of the letter or letters left out. Many contractions are made from a verb and the word *not*.

Example: do not/<u>don't</u> (An apostrophe takes the place of the *o* in *not*.)

Unusual spellings: cannot/<u>can't</u>; will not/<u>won't</u>

Contraction Action!

Write the two words from which each contraction is made.

1. wouldn't _____   2. haven't _____

3. aren't _____   4. doesn't _____

Write the contraction for each pair of words.

5. had not _____   6. did not _____

7. should not _____   8. has not _____

Some **contractions** are made by joining a pronoun and a linking verb.
An **apostrophe** (') is used in place of the letter or letters left out.
Example: I am/I'<u>m</u> (An apostrophe takes the place of the *a* in *am*.)

Some contractions are made by joining a pronoun with *will* or *would*.
Examples: I will/I'<u>ll</u> (An apostrophe takes the place of the *wi* in *will*.)
I would/I'<u>d</u> (An apostrophe takes the place of the *woul* in *would*.)

Write the two words from which each contraction is made.

9. she'll _____   10. he'd _____

11. you've _____   12. she's _____

Write the contraction for each pair of words.

13. you are _____   14. she would _____

15. they have _____   16. he will _____

Name

Read or listen to the directions. Fill in the circle beside the best answer.

❑ Example:

Which word is not a present tense action verb?

(A) march

(B) compete

(C) have

(D) stand

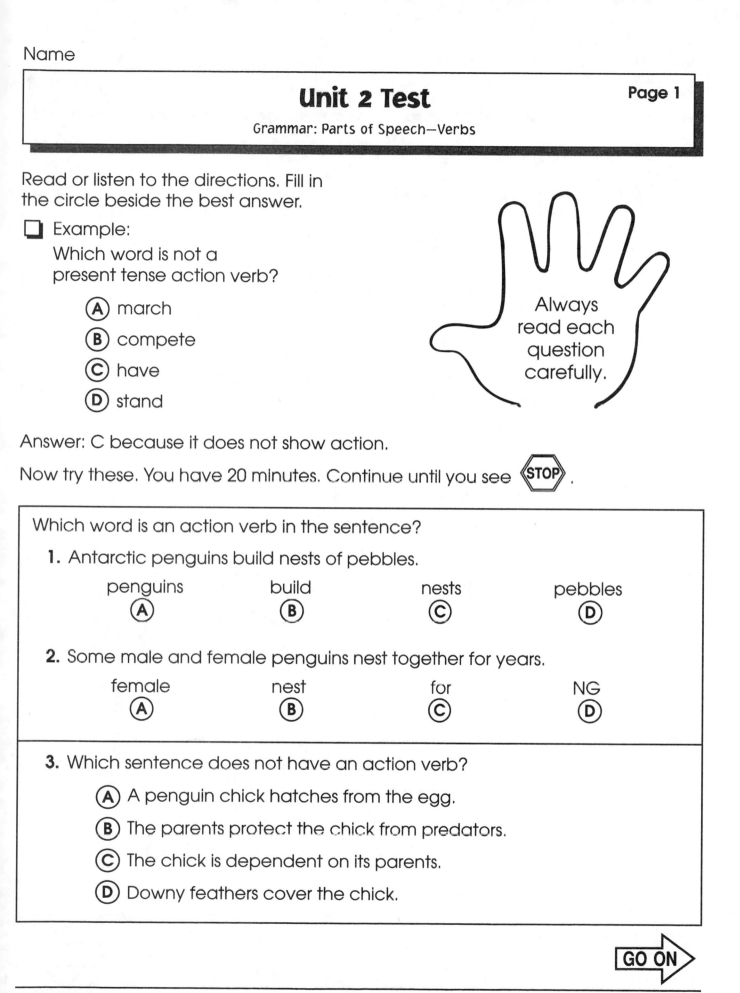

Always read each question carefully.

Answer: C because it does not show action.

Now try these. You have 20 minutes. Continue until you see ⬡STOP .

Which word is an action verb in the sentence?

1. Antarctic penguins build nests of pebbles.

penguins	build	nests	pebbles
(A)	(B)	(C)	(D)

2. Some male and female penguins nest together for years.

female	nest	for	NG
(A)	(B)	(C)	(D)

3. Which sentence does not have an action verb?

(A) A penguin chick hatches from the egg.

(B) The parents protect the chick from predators.

(C) The chick is dependent on its parents.

(D) Downy feathers cover the chick.

GO ON ⟹

Which word is a linking verb in the sentence?

4. Baleen whales have horny plates in their mouth.

whales
(A)

have
(B)

in
(C)

their
(D)

5. Female baleen whales are larger than males.

are
(A)

larger
(B)

than
(C)

males
(D)

6. Which sentence does not have a linking verb?

(A) Whales have no sense of smell.

(B) Whales hear very well.

(C) A whale has only tiny ear openings.

(D) Most mammals have four limbs.

Which is the correct past tense of the action verb?

7. study

studyed
(A)

studyied
(B)

studied
(C)

studyd
(D)

8. flip

flipt
(A)

fliped
(B)

flipied
(C)

NG
(D)

9. Which sentence does not have a past tense action verb?

(A) The gorilla walked on all fours through the jungle.

(B) Then it climbed a tree to rest and eat.

(C) Gorillas are usually quiet animals.

(D) The male grumbled softly.

GO ON

10. Which sentence does not have a past tense linking verb?

Ⓐ Scolosaurus had spikes over most of its body.

Ⓑ It also had plates over most of its body.

Ⓒ Its body was low and wide.

Ⓓ Scolosaurus protected itself very well.

Which word is a present tense irregular verb?

11. know Ⓐ   next Ⓑ   nectar Ⓒ   hunt Ⓓ

12. shower Ⓐ   shoot Ⓑ   skate Ⓒ   smile Ⓓ

13. Which sentence has a present tense irregular verb?

Ⓐ The cheetah follows the target.

Ⓑ The cheetah strikes the impala with a forepaw.

Ⓒ It knocks her prey off its feet.

Ⓓ It clamps the impala's throat in her jaws.

14. Which word is a past tense irregular verb?

war Ⓐ   warn Ⓑ   knew Ⓒ   NG Ⓓ

15. Which sentence does not have a past tense irregular verb?

    (A) Egyptians built pyramids more than 4,500 years ago.

    (B) Workers used over two million limestone blocks on just one pyramid!

    (C) It took 20 years to finish the Great Pyramid.

    (C) They knew it would be impressive.

16. Which sentence has a helping verb and a main verb?

    (A) Some planets have moons that revolve around them.

    (B) Earth has just one moon.

    (C) Scientists have photographed the two moons of Mars.

    (D) Europa is one of Jupiter's moons.

Does the underlined verb tell about the past, present, or future?

17. The female cricket <u>laid</u> her eggs in holes in the ground.

    past   present   future

    (A)   (B)   (C)

18. The eggs <u>will hatch</u> in the spring.

    past   present   future

    (A)   (B)   (C)

19. What is the contraction for **are not**?

    are'nt   arenot'   aren't   arent'

    (A)   (B)   (C)   (D)

20. Which sentence does not have a contraction?

(A) Shelly's new bike is a cross-bike.

(B) She'll be able to use it on roads and trails.

(C) She isn't able to ride it until Tuesday.

(D) Shelly can't wait to ride it.

Which verb—**plays, played, will play**—belongs in this sentence? Give your reason for choosing it.

Lamar _____ in the school orchestra next year.

_____

_____

Name _____

Adjectives

An **adjective** is a word that describes a noun. It can tell how many or what kind. An adjective often comes in front of the noun it describes.
Example: Lou raises <u>fifty</u> llamas on his ranch. (<u>Fifty</u> tells how many.)

An adjective can come after a linking verb. A linking verb connects the subject part of a sentence with an adjective in the predicate.
Example: Llamas are <u>lovable</u>. (<u>Lovable</u> tells what kind.)

A sentence may have more than one adjective.
Example: Lou raises <u>fifty lovable</u> llamas on his ranch.

Lou's Llamas

Write the adjective or adjectives that describe each noun in **bold** type. (Do not include articles.)

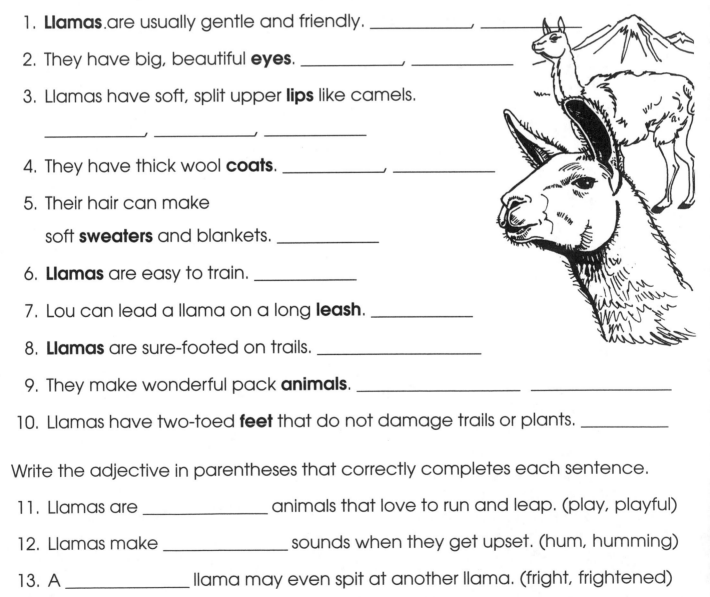

1. **Llamas** are usually gentle and friendly. _____, _____

2. They have big, beautiful **eyes**. _____, _____

3. Llamas have soft, split upper **lips** like camels.

   _____, _____, _____

4. They have thick wool **coats**. _____, _____

5. Their hair can make

   soft **sweaters** and blankets. _____

6. **Llamas** are easy to train. _____

7. Lou can lead a llama on a long **leash**. _____

8. **Llamas** are sure-footed on trails. _____

9. They make wonderful pack **animals**. _____ _____

10. Llamas have two-toed **feet** that do not damage trails or plants. _____

Write the adjective in parentheses that correctly completes each sentence.

11. Llamas are _____ animals that love to run and leap. (play, playful)

12. Llamas make _____ sounds when they get upset. (hum, humming)

13. A _____ llama may even spit at another llama. (fright, frightened)

Adjectives
Unit 3

An **adjective** is a word that describes a noun. It can tell how many or what kind.
An adjective often comes in front of the noun it describes.
Example: I see a <u>tall</u> tree. (<u>Tall</u> tells what kind.)

An **adjective** can come after a linking verb. A linking verb links the subject part
of a sentence with an adjective in the predicate. Example: The tree is <u>old</u>.
(*Is* links the *tree* in the subject with the adjective <u>old</u> in the predicate.)

A sentence may have more than one adjective. Example: The <u>tall</u> tree is <u>old</u>.

Marvelous Maple Syrup

Write the adjective or adjectives that describe each noun in **bold** type. (Do not
include articles.)

1. Many **people** enjoy eating pancakes with maple syrup. _____

2. Maple **syrup** is sweet and delicious. _____, _____, _____

3. It is a product of the sugar maple **tree**. _____, _____

4. Pure maple **sugar** is expensive. _____, _____, _____

5. It takes nearly 40 **gallons** of sap to make a gallon of syrup. _____

6. The **sap** is colorless and watery. _____, _____

7. It is boiled in long, shallow **pans**. _____, _____

8. The water evaporates, and the pure maple **sugar** remains.
   _____, _____

9. Its flavor and golden brown **color** are
   developed during this process.

   _____, _____

10. Because pure maple sugar is
    expensive, artificial maple **flavorings**
    are used in some syrups.

    _____, _____

Adjectives that compare   Unit 3

An **adjective** is used to compare persons, places, and things. Add **-er** to most adjectives when comparing two nouns. Add **-est** to most adjectives when comparing more than two nouns. Example: near/near<u>er</u>/near<u>est</u>

If the adjective ends in silent **-e**, drop the **-e** before adding **-er** or **-est**. Example: white/whit<u>er</u>/whit<u>est</u>

If a one-syllable adjective has a consonant-vowel-consonant pattern, double the final consonant before adding **-er** or **-est**. Example: thin/thin<u>ner</u>/thin<u>nest</u>

If a adjective ends in **-y**, change the **-y** to **-i** and add **-er** or **-est**. Example: shiny/shin<u>ier</u>/shin<u>iest</u>

Use **more** before most adjectives that have more than two syllables to compare two nouns. Use **most** before most adjectives that have more than two syllables to compare more than two nouns. Example: beautiful/<u>more</u> beautiful/<u>most</u> beautiful

Use **more** and **most** with some two-syllable adjectives that do not use **-er** endings. Example: awful/<u>more</u> awful/<u>most</u> awful

Dig This!

Follow the rules above to complete the chart with forms of each adjective that can compare nouns.

Adjectives	Adjectives That Compare Two Nouns	Adjectives That Compare More Than Two Nouns
1. crumbly	_____	_____
2. flat	_____	_____
3. brave	_____	_____
4. convenient	_____	_____
5. graceful	_____	_____
6. effective	_____	_____
7. needy	_____	_____

Underline the correct adjective to complete each sentence.

8. Some archaeological digs can be (more dangerous, most dangerous) than others.

9. Remote jungle sites may be (dangerous, more dangerous).

10. The (more dangerous, most dangerous) dig Dr. Lee ever went on was to Peru.

Name

Predicate adjectives, proper adjectives, and proper nouns

A **predicate adjective** is an adjective used after a linking verb to describe the subject of the sentence. Example: Our flag is <u>beautiful</u>. (<u>Beautiful</u> describes the flag.)

A **proper adjective** is a word made from a **proper noun**. It is used to describe a noun. It begins with a capital letter. Example: The <u>Missouri</u> flag flies over the capitol in Jefferson City. (<u>Missouri</u> is a proper noun, but here it is used as an adjective to describe the flag.)

A **proper adjective** can be formed by adding an ending to a **proper noun**. It begins with a capital letter. Example: The <u>American</u> flag flies over the capitol in Washington, D. C. (<u>American</u> is made from the proper noun *America*.)

Flag Facts

Read each sentence. Write **1** if the word in bold type is a predicate adjective, **2** if the word is a proper adjective, or **3** if the word is a proper noun.

_____ 1. Flags are **important** to nations, states, organizations, and people.

_____ 2. The **Chinese** people used silk flags as long ago as 3000 B.C.

_____ 3. National flags were first used in **Europe** and North America in the 1700s.

_____ 4. The *Stars and Stripes* is a "nickname" for the **United States** flag.

_____ 5. The **American** flag is also called *Old Glory*.

_____ 6. The **Swiss** flag features a white cross on a red background.

_____ 7. The flag of the **Red Cross** is the reverse—a red cross on a white field.

_____ 8. Many nations' flags are **colorful** with striking designs and symbols.

_____ 9. Some flags used in **Arab** nations show the eagle of Saladin.

_____ 10. A nation's flag is **symbolic** of its people, its government, and its ideals.

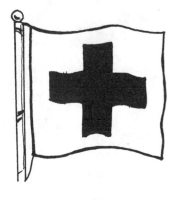  

Articles   Unit 3

A, **an**, and **the** are special adjectives called **articles**. Use **a** to describe any singular noun that begins with a consonant sound. Use **an** to describe **any singular noun** that begins with a vowel sound. Use **the** with singular or plural nouns to tell about a particular person, place, or thing.

Examples: <u>a</u> house, <u>an</u> apartment, <u>the</u> library

This Must Be the Place

Write **a** or **an** in front of each singular noun.
Write **the** in front of each plural noun.

1. _____ igloo

2. _____ temple

3. _____ tower

4. _____ cellar

5. _____ station

6. _____ museums

7. _____ chapels

8. _____ cottages

9. _____ apartment

10. _____ fort

11. _____ courthouse

12. _____ auditorium

13. _____ colleges

14. _____ grocery

Sometimes the noun is preceded by one or more adjectives. Use **a** in front of an adjective that begins with a consonant sound. Example: <u>a</u> large apartment (The article no longer precedes the noun beginning with a vowel, so use <u>a,</u> not *an*.)

Use **an** in front of an adjective that begins with a vowel sound. Example: <u>an</u> unusual building (The article no longer precedes the noun beginning with a consonant sound, so use <u>an</u>, not *a*.)

Use the articles **a** and **an** correctly with each phrase below.

15. _____ huge skyscraper

16. _____ empty arena

17. _____ ugly building

18. _____ grand hotel

19. _____ old cabin

20. _____ hot, dusty attic

21. _____ brand-new store

22. _____ outstanding bakery

23. _____ cozy home

24. _____ lovely office

Name

Adverbs

Unit 3

An **adverb** is a word that tells how, when, or where the action of the verb takes place. Adverbs that tell how usually end in **-ly**.

Examples: Kara <u>cheerfully</u> went <u>outdoors</u> <u>yesterday</u>.
          (how)   (where)   (when)

Give a Cheer!

Identify each adverb below as one that tells how, when, or where. Circle the correct answer.

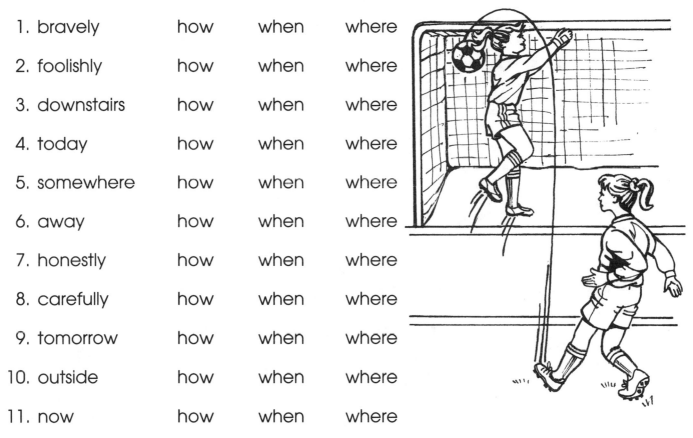

1. bravely   how   when   where

2. foolishly   how   when   where

3. downstairs   how   when   where

4. today   how   when   where

5. somewhere   how   when   where

6. away   how   when   where

7. honestly   how   when   where

8. carefully   how   when   where

9. tomorrow   how   when   where

10. outside   how   when   where

11. now   how   when   where

Complete each sentence with an adverb that tells how, when, or where.

12. Kara wanted to play soccer _____ . (when)

13. She _____ ran to the field. (how)

14. She waited _____ for the rest of her friends to arrive. (where)

15. The game started _____. (when)

16. Everyone cheered _____ when Kara scored a goal. (how)

Name

Adverbs   Unit 3

An **adverb** is a word that tells how, when, or where the action of the verb takes place.
Adverbs that tell how usually end in **-ly**.

Examples: <u>Yesterday</u> Paul <u>earnestly</u> began looking <u>here</u> for fossils.
        (when)   (how)   (where)

On the Trail of the Trilobites

Write the one or two adverbs that describe the action of the underlined verb in each sentence.

1. The paleontologist <u>looked</u> down at the ground. _____

2. Paul <u>found</u> some brownish, oval-shaped rocks there. _____

3. He <u>chose</u> one rock carefully. _____

4. He cautiously <u>brushed</u> the soil away. _____, _____

5. Paul <u>tapped</u> the rock gently with his coal hammer. _____

6. It neatly <u>split</u> into two pieces. _____

7. Then the paleontologist <u>saw</u> the fossil of a trilobite. _____

8. Trilobites once <u>swam</u> freely in the oceans. _____, _____

9. They <u>lived</u> everywhere in the oceans during the Cambrian period. _____

10. Trilobites <u>varied</u> in size greatly. _____

11. Next Paul <u>gathered</u> other rocks nearby. _____, _____

12. He <u>took</u> them back to his lab to crack open later. _____, _____

Choose one adverb from above
that tells how, one that tells when,
and one that tells where. Then
use all three in a sentence.

Name

Adverbs: comparative and superlative

An **adverb** is a word that tells how, when, or where the action of the verb takes place. Add **-er** to one-syllable adverbs to compare two actions. Add **-est** to one-syllable adverbs to compare more than two actions. Examples: Jill ran <u>fast</u>. Janell ran <u>faster</u> than Jill. Julie ran <u>fastest</u> of all.

Adverbs often end in **-ly**. Use **more** before these adverbs to compare two actions. Use **most** when comparing more than two actions. Examples: Julie dances <u>gracefully</u>. Janell dances <u>more gracefully</u> than Julie. Jill dances <u>most gracefully</u> of all.

Sooner or Later

Follow the rules above to complete the chart with forms of each adverb that compare the action of verbs.

Adverbs	Adverbs That Compare Two Actions	Adverbs That Compare More Than Two Actions
1. quietly	_____	_____
2. hard	_____	_____
3. frequently	_____	_____
4. long	_____	_____
5. close	_____	_____
6. patiently	_____	_____
7. soon	_____	_____

Complete each sentence with the correct adverb in parentheses.

8. Mom, Ted, and I _____ waited for Dad to arrive. (patiently, more patiently)

9. We _____ looked out the front window. (eagerly, most eagerly)

10. _____ Dad drove up the driveway. (Soon, Sooner)

11. I ran to the car _____ than my sister. (more quickly, most quickly)

12. Dad smiled _____ as he took a basket out of the car. (broadly, most broadly)

13. The new puppy yelped _____! (loudly, more loudly)

Name _____

Read or listen to the directions. Fill in the circle beside the best answer.

🔲 Example:

Which word is an adjective in this sentence?

Tommy quickly ran under the big tree.

quickly   ran   under   big
Ⓐ   Ⓑ   Ⓒ   Ⓓ

Answer: D because it describes the noun *tree*.

Now try these. You have 20 minutes. Continue until you see ⬡STOP .

Read all the answer choices before you choose the one you think is correct.

Which word is an adjective in the sentence?

1. Pigs have flat noses called snouts.

have   flat   called   snouts
Ⓐ   Ⓑ   Ⓒ   Ⓓ

2. Pigs are very smart animals.

very   smart   animals   are
Ⓐ   Ⓑ   Ⓒ   Ⓓ

---

3. Which sentence does not have an adjective?

Ⓐ A manatee is a mammal.

Ⓑ This gray creature lives in water.

Ⓒ It has a wrinkled face.

Ⓓ Its flippers are short.

GO ON

Name

4. Which word is not an adjective?

A manatee has a rounded tail and no hind legs.

rounded	hind	no	NG
Ⓐ	Ⓑ	Ⓒ	Ⓓ

Choose an adjective that describes each noun.

5. house

through	because	charming	there
Ⓐ	Ⓑ	Ⓒ	Ⓓ

6. plate

delicate	around	quickly	break
Ⓐ	Ⓑ	Ⓒ	Ⓓ

Choose the correct form of the adjective to complete the sentence.

7. Mexico City is _____ than New York City.

large	larger	largest	most larger
Ⓐ	Ⓑ	Ⓒ	Ⓓ

8. Ramon thinks New York City is the ___ city in all of the United States.

beautiful	more beautiful	most beautiful	beautifuler
Ⓐ	Ⓑ	Ⓒ	Ⓓ

9. In which phrase is the article used incorrectly?

an onion	the apple	an pear	a lemon
Ⓐ	Ⓑ	Ⓒ	Ⓓ

10. In which phrase is the article used incorrectly?

a large anteater	an angry lion	a unusual bird	a playful bear
Ⓐ	Ⓑ	Ⓒ	Ⓓ

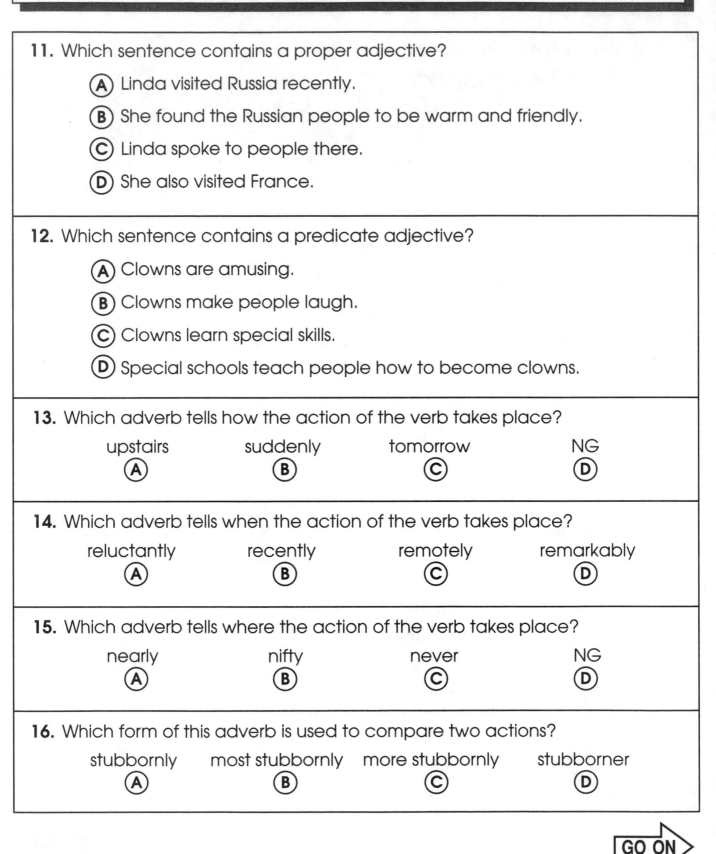

11. Which sentence contains a proper adjective?

(A) Linda visited Russia recently.

(B) She found the Russian people to be warm and friendly.

(C) Linda spoke to people there.

(D) She also visited France.

12. Which sentence contains a predicate adjective?

(A) Clowns are amusing.

(B) Clowns make people laugh.

(C) Clowns learn special skills.

(D) Special schools teach people how to become clowns.

13. Which adverb tells how the action of the verb takes place?

upstairs (A)   suddenly (B)   tomorrow (C)   NG (D)

14. Which adverb tells when the action of the verb takes place?

reluctantly (A)   recently (B)   remotely (C)   remarkably (D)

15. Which adverb tells where the action of the verb takes place?

nearly (A)   nifty (B)   never (C)   NG (D)

16. Which form of this adverb is used to compare two actions?

stubbornly (A)   most stubbornly (B)   more stubbornly (C)   stubborner (D)

GO ON

17. Which sentence does not contain an adverb?

(A) Tomorrow Carlos begins a new job.

(B) Carlos will be a school crossing guard.

(C) He takes his responsibilities seriously.

(D) The police trained him carefully.

18. In which sentence is the adverb used incorrectly?

(A) Yesterday was the first snowfall of the season.

(B) The snow fell more rapidly.

(C) It quickly covered the countryside.

(D) We must drive carefully to town.

19. Which form of this adverb is used to compare more than two actions?

most eagerly   eagerly   eagerer   more eagerly
(A)   (B)   (C)   (D)

20. Identify the part of speech of the underlined word.

Hal <u>cautiously</u> opened the attic door.

predicate adjective   adjective   adverb   verb
(A)   (B)   (C)   (D)

Which adverb—**rapidly, more rapidly, most rapidly**—correctly completes this sentence? Write your reason for choosing it.

Dantae finished the test _____ than Andrew.

_____

_____

STOP

Four kinds of sentences   Unit 4

There are four kinds of sentences: **declarative**, **interrogative**, **exclamatory**, and **imperative**.

A **declarative sentence**, also called a statement, tells a complete thought. It ends with a period (.). Example: Hector is on the track team.

An **interrogative sentence**, also called a question, asks something. It ends with a question mark (?). Example: What event does Hector run?

An **exclamatory sentence** shows great emotion. It ends with an exclamation mark (!). An exclamatory sentence often begins or ends with an interjection such as *wow*. The interjection is separated from the rest of the sentence by a comma. Example: The mile, wow!

An **imperative sentence**, also called a command, gives an order. It ends with a period (.). Example: Take me to the next track meet.

Roger, the Racer

Identify each of the following sentences. Write **D** for a declarative sentence, **INT** for an interrogative sentence, **E** for an exclamatory sentence, or **IMP** for an imperative sentence. Add the correct ending mark.

_____ 1. May 6, 1954, is an important day in the history of track and field

_____ 2. Why do you say that

_____ 3. The world record in the mile race was broken on that day

_____ 4. Tell me more about the race

_____ 5. Until then, no one had ever run a mile in less than four minutes

_____ 6. What had been the world record

_____ 7. Four minutes and one second—that is really fast

_____ 8. That time was set in 1945 by a Swedish runner

_____ 9. Go on with the story

_____ 10. An Englishman named Roger Bannister was a great runner

_____ 11. Was his dream to break the four-minute-mile barrier

_____ 12. Yes, and on May 6, 1954, he ran the mile in under four minutes

_____ 13. That is absolutely amazing

_____ 14. How long did his record last

_____ 15. It was broken just seven weeks later by an Australian, John Landry

Name _____

Declarative and imperative sentences

A **declarative sentence**, also called a statement, tells a complete thought. It ends with a period (.). Example: Geology is the study of the earth.

An **imperative sentence**, also called a command, gives an order. There is no written or spoken subject in an imperative sentence, however *you*, both singular and plural, is the implied subject. The sentence ends with a period (.). Examples: (You) Find out what a geologist does. (All of you) Read a book about geology.

Scientific Studies

Identify each sentence as either a declarative sentence or an imperative sentence.
Write **D** for declarative or **I** for imperative.

_____ 1. Geologists are scientists who study the origin, history, and structure of the earth.

_____ 2. Some geologists are called paleontologists.

_____ 3. Paleontologists study plant and animal fossils.

_____ 4. Read about discoveries made by paleontologists.

_____ 5. Look for more information in the library and on the Internet.

_____ 6. Some geologists search for oil and gas in the oceans and on land.

_____ 7. Explain why petroleum is important.

_____ 8. Gasoline and home heating oil come from petroleum.

_____ 9. Geologists also work on space exploration projects.

_____ 10. Find out what they have discovered about the moon.

Pretend you are teaching a science class on a subject of interest to you, other than geology. Write three imperative sentences giving your students their assignments for the lesson. Use a different verb in each sentence.

Name

Interrogative and exclamatory sentences   Unit 4

An **interrogative** sentence asks a question. It ends with a question mark (**?**).
Example: What is an iceberg?

An **exclamatory sentence** shows great emotion. It ends with an exclamation mark (**!**).
An exclamatory sentence often begins or ends with an interjection, such as *wow*.
The interjection is separated from the rest of the sentence by a comma.
Example: Wow, some weigh a million tons!

Awesome Icebergs!

Identify each sentence as either an interrogative sentence or an exclamatory
sentence. Write **I** for interrogative or **E** for exclamatory. Add the correct ending
marks.

_____ 1. Are icebergs huge chunks of ice

_____ 2. Do they break off a glacier and fall into the ocean

_____ 3. Oh my, the cracking ice sounds like an explosion

_____ 4. That is awesome

_____ 5. What are "bergy bits"

_____ 6. Golly, pieces of icebergs the size of a house

_____ 7. Can you tell me about icebergs in Antarctica

_____ 8. Are they usually bigger than those in the North Atlantic

_____ 9. How long was the largest iceberg ever seen

_____ 10. Two-hundred miles long, wow

Write 10 words that are often used to begin questions. _____

_____

Write three questions about icebergs that have not been asked in the sentences
above. Begin each question with a different word from your list of 10 words.

1. _____

2. _____

3. _____

Sentences, fragments, and run-ons

A **declarative sentence** tells a complete thought. Example: Venus is a planet.

A **fragment** does not tell a complete thought. Example: From the sun.

A **run-on sentence** has too many thoughts, often strung together with commas. The thoughts are not connected correctly with a conjunction or with the correct punctuation. Example: Venus's distance from the sun is about 67.2 miles, Earth's distance from the sun is about 93 million miles, Mercury is the closest planet to the sun.

Earth's Twin

Write **D** for declarative sentence, **F** for fragment, or **R** for run-on.

_____ 1. Venus and Earth are similar in size.

_____ 2. Called Earth's twin.

_____ 3. Venus's diameter is only 400 miles smaller than Earth's.

_____ 4. About 25.7 million miles away from Earth.

_____ 5. Venus looks brighter than other planets and stars from Earth, it can be seen in the western sky in the evening at certain times of the year, it can be seen in the eastern sky in the morning at other times.

_____ 6. Ancient astronomers named the planet Venus.

_____ 7. After the Roman goddess of love and beauty.

_____ 8. Venus is always surrounded by clouds.

_____ 9. The surface of the planet is hot and dry.

_____ 10. Mountains, canyons, and valleys.

_____ 11. Over half its surface is flat and covered with thousands of volcanoes.

_____ 12. Venus orbits the sun once every 225 Earth days, it takes Earth 365 days, its orbit is nearly circular, the other planets have oval-shaped orbits.

Rewrite one of the above run-on sentences to make several better declarative sentences.

_____

_____

_____

Name

Simple subjects and predicates

A declarative sentence has a subject that tells who or what the statement is about. It has a noun or pronoun that is called the **simple subject**. Example: <u>Many people</u> enjoy winter sports. (The complete subject is underlined. *People* is the simple subject.)

A declarative sentence has a predicate that tells what the subject does or is. It contains an action verb or a linking verb that is called the **simple predicate**.
Example: Skiers <u>glide over snow on skis</u>. (The complete predicate is underlined. *Glide* is the simple predicate.)

Fun in the Snow

Circle the simple subject and underline the simple predicate in each sentence.

1. A snowmobile is a motorized sled.

2. One or two persons ride on a snowmobile.

3. The driver steers with handlebars.

4. Snowmobiles are capable of traveling over 50 miles per hour.

5. Some environmentalists believe snowmobiling harms nature and animals.

6. Another kind of sled is a toboggan.

7. Toboggans are long wooden sleds without runners.

8. Highly polished wood allows toboggans to coast over ice and snow.

9. Usually four people ride a toboggan in competitions.

10. A driver steers the toboggan from the rear.

11. Snowboarding became a popular winter sport in the 1980s.

12. Snowboards look similar to skateboards without wheels.

13. A snowboarder does many of the same movements as skiers.

14. Snowboarding became an Olympic event in 1998.

On another sheet of paper, write four sentences about a winter sport you know about or one that you enjoy. Circle the simple subject and underline the simple predicate in each of your four sentences.

Name

Complete subjects

The subject of a sentence tells who or what the sentence is about. The **complete subject** contains a noun or pronoun, called the simple subject, and any words that complement it.

Example: <u>The animal with the largest ears</u> is the African elephant. (The complete subject is underlined. The simple subject is *animal*.)

It's a Fact!

Underline the complete subject. Circle the simple subject.

1. A giant tortoise may live a hundred years.

2. Baby pandas are completely white at birth.

3. These mammals spend 12 hours a day eating.

4. An alligator's eye has three eyelids.

5. Giraffes have the same number of neck bones as humans.

6. A sloth may spend its whole life in just one tree.

7. An elephant's trunk has 40,000 muscles.

8. An octopus is a shy sea creature.

9. Octopuses grow new tentacles if they lose any.

10. A chameleon's tongue is as long as its body.

11. Dolphin brains weigh more than human brains.

12. A hummingbird can fly straight up.

13. A horse's hoof is really a toe.

14. A camel is born without a hump.

15. The world's largest birds are ostriches.

16. Young gorillas play games human boys and girls play.

 On another sheet of paper, write four sentences about animals, each with a different subject. Underline the complete subjects and circle the simple subjects.

Name

Complete predicates

The predicate of a sentence tells what the subject does or is. The **complete predicate** contains an action verb or a linking verb, called the simple predicate, and any words that complement it.

Example: Sonny <u>is a tree squirrel</u>. (The complete predicate is underlined. *Is*, a linking verb, is the simple predicate.)

Sonny Squirrel

Underline each complete predicate with two lines. Circle the simple predicate.

1. Sonny Squirrel lives in a nest high in an old elm tree.

2. Sonny awakens in his leafy nest early in the morning.

3. The rest of Sonny's family left earlier to look for food.

4. Sonny races along the elm's branches.

5. The squirrel scampers down the tree trunk.

6. Sonny searches for some seeds he had buried.

7. His good sense of smell helps him find them.

8. The squirrel spies his brothers nearby.

9. They chatter back and forth.

10. Then they chase one another all around.

11. Soon Sonny tires of the game.

12. He stretches out in the warm sun to rest.

Write a predicate for each subject below to continue the story of Sonny Squirrel. Use a different action verb or linking verb in each predicate.

13. Next, Sonny _____

14. He _____

15. The squirrels _____

16. Finally, Sonny _____

Name

Compound subjects and compound predicates

A **compound subject** has two or more simple subjects joined by *and*.
Example: The <u>climate</u> *and* <u>vegetation</u> began to change at the end of the Ice Age.
(The sentence has two simple subjects.)

A **compound predicate** has two or more simple predicates joined by *and*. Example: Trees
<u>grew</u> *and* <u>covered</u> the land with thick forests. (The sentence has two simple predicates.)

Stone Age Farmers

Read each sentence. Write **CS** if the sentence has a compound subject. Write **CP** if it has a compound predicate. Write **N** if the sentence has neither a compound subject nor a compound predicate.

_____ 1. Stone Age farmers cut the trees and cleared the forests.

_____ 2. They used stone axes and picks.

_____ 3. Wood and deer antlers were used for handles.

_____ 4. Tree trunks and large branches were used to build shelters.

_____ 5. People also made canoes from the tree trunks.

_____ 6. People, animals, and crops needed water to survive.

_____ 7. Communities were often started near rivers or lakes.

_____ 8. People caught fish and traveled on the water.

_____ 9. Stone Age people used fire for cooking and warmth.

_____ 10. They rubbed two pieces of flint together and made a spark to start a fire.

_____ 11. Farmers harvested their crops and kept seed for planting next year.

_____ 12. Hunting and fishing were still important to farmers.

_____ 13. They needed more food than they could grow.

Write two declarative sentences about farming today. Use a compound subject in one sentence and a compound predicate in the other.

_____

_____

Name

Compound sentences

Use **and** to combine two sentences when their thoughts complement each other.
Example: Gordie Howe was an outstanding hockey player. Wayne Gretzky was magnificent, also.
Gordie Howe was an outstanding hockey player, and Wayne Gretzky was magnificent, also.

Use **but** to combine two sentences with contrasting thoughts. Example: Gordie Howe scored 801 goals in 26 seasons. Wayne Gretzky scored more. Gordie Howe scored 801 goals in 26 seasons, but Wayne Gretzky scored more.

(Notice that the period at the end of each first sentence has been replaced with a comma, followed by *and* or *but*.)

Hockey Greats

Combine each pair of sentences to write a compound sentence.

1. Gordie Howe was known as "Mr. Hockey." Wayne Gretzky was called "The Great One."

   _____

   _____

2. Howe joined the Detroit Red Wings in 1946. Gretzky began playing professionally in 1978.

   _____

   _____

3. Howe spent most of his hockey career with the Red Wings. Gretzky played with several different teams.

   _____

   _____

4. Howe played right wing. Gretzky was a center.

   _____

5. Gordie Howe played hockey for 26 seasons. Wayne Gretzky only played for 20 seasons.

   _____

   _____

Word order in sentences   Unit 4

Words in a sentence must be in the **correct order** to make sense.

Example: nine planets has the known sun. (This sentence does not make sense.)

Example: The sun has nine known planets. (Changing the order of the same words makes the sentence make sense.)

Sensational Saturn

Write each group of words in the correct order to form a declarative sentence.

1. Seven moons that orbit them have planets.

   _____

2. Their own light do not have planets.

   _____

3. Many rings it has around Saturn.

   _____

The **order of words** in a sentence can determine whether a sentence is a declarative sentence or an interrogative sentence.

Example: The sun does have nine known planets. (The order of the words makes this a declarative sentence.)

Example: Does the sun have nine known planets? (The order of these same words makes this an interrogative sentence.)

Reorder the words in each declarative sentence to write an interrogative sentence.

4. Saturn is the second largest planet.

   _____

5. You can see Saturn's rings with a telescope.

   _____

6. Saturn's biggest moon was first seen in 1655.

   _____

Name

Read or listen to the directions. Fill in the circle beside the best answer.

☐ Example:

What kind of sentence is the sentence below?

Turn in your report Monday.

(A) declarative

(B) interrogative

(C) imperative

(D) exclamatory

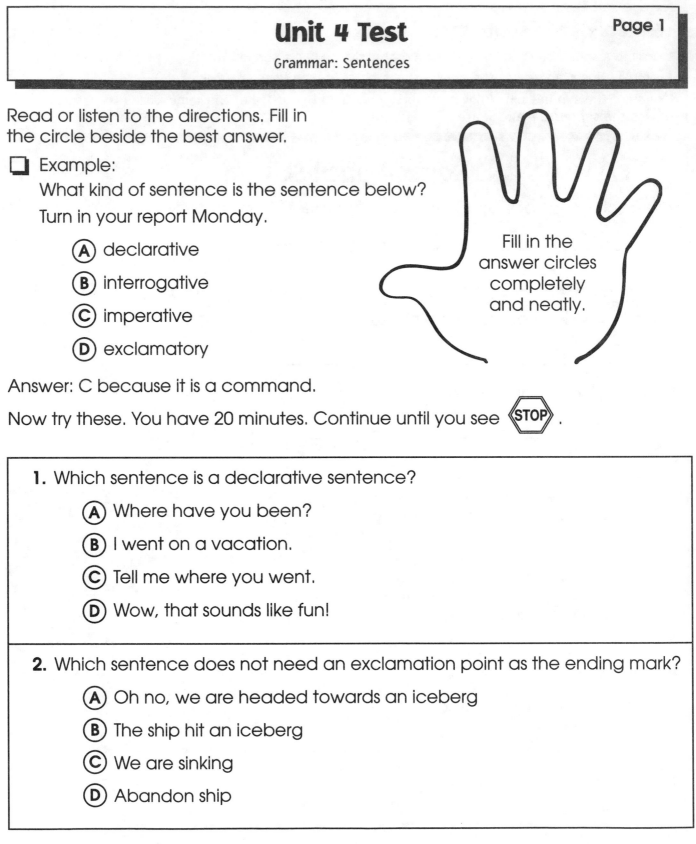

Fill in the answer circles completely and neatly.

Answer: C because it is a command.

Now try these. You have 20 minutes. Continue until you see ⬡STOP .

---

1. Which sentence is a declarative sentence?

(A) Where have you been?

(B) I went on a vacation.

(C) Tell me where you went.

(D) Wow, that sounds like fun!

---

2. Which sentence does not need an exclamation point as the ending mark?

(A) Oh no, we are headed towards an iceberg

(B) The ship hit an iceberg

(C) We are sinking

(D) Abandon ship

GO ON

3. Which sentence is an imperative sentence?

(A) What are you looking at with that telescope?

(B) I am trying to find Venus.

(C) Incredible, I found it!

(D) Let me take a look for it.

4. Which sentence is not an interrogative sentence?

(A) Hurry up, or we will be late!

(B) What time does the movie begin?

(C) Can we go to a later showing?

(D) How long is the movie?

5. Why is this sentence an interrogative sentence?

When are your library books due?

(A) It is a statement.

(B) It gives a command.

(C) It shows great emotion.

(D) It asks a question.

6. Which is not a complete sentence?

(A) Old Faithful is a famous geyser.

(B) It blows water and steam into the air.

(C) Sometimes the water and steam reach 180 feet.

(D) Yellowstone National Park.

GO ON

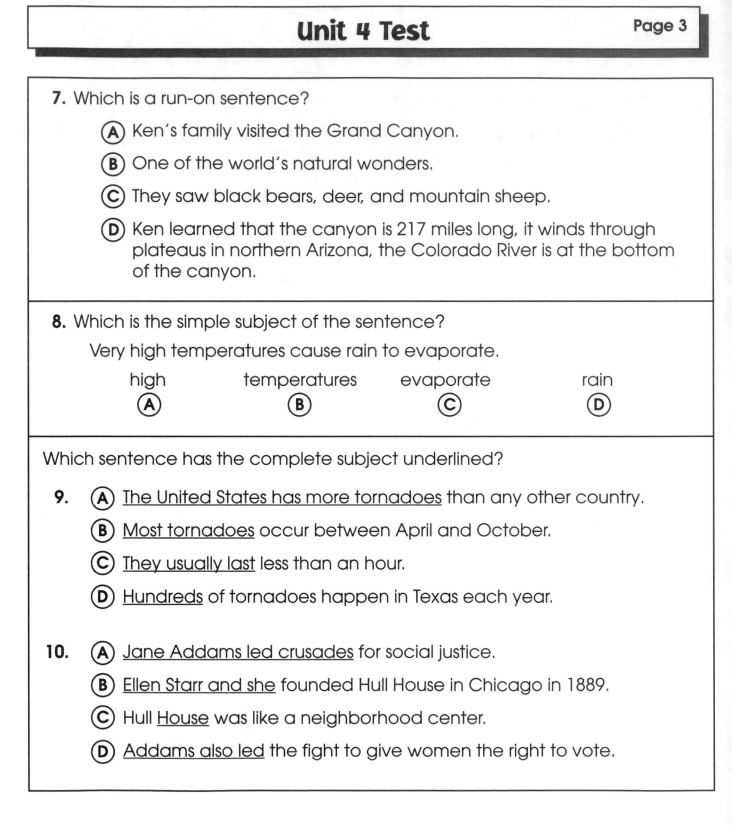

7. Which is a run-on sentence?

   Ⓐ Ken's family visited the Grand Canyon.

   Ⓑ One of the world's natural wonders.

   Ⓒ They saw black bears, deer, and mountain sheep.

   Ⓓ Ken learned that the canyon is 217 miles long, it winds through plateaus in northern Arizona, the Colorado River is at the bottom of the canyon.

8. Which is the simple subject of the sentence?

   Very high temperatures cause rain to evaporate.

high	temperatures	evaporate	rain
Ⓐ	Ⓑ	Ⓒ	Ⓓ

Which sentence has the complete subject underlined?

9.   Ⓐ The United States has more tornadoes than any other country.

   Ⓑ Most tornadoes occur between April and October.

   Ⓒ They usually last less than an hour.

   Ⓓ Hundreds of tornadoes happen in Texas each year.

10.   Ⓐ Jane Addams led crusades for social justice.

   Ⓑ Ellen Starr and she founded Hull House in Chicago in 1889.

   Ⓒ Hull House was like a neighborhood center.

   Ⓓ Addams also led the fight to give women the right to vote.

GO ON

11. What is the simple predicate of the sentence?

A tornado is a powerful, twisting storm.

tornado
(A)

powerful
(B)

is
(C)

storm
(D)

Which sentence has the complete predicate underlined?

12. (A) The Stone Age refers <u>to a time about 2 ½ million years ago</u>.

(B) Stone Age <u>people cooked their food several ways</u>.

(C) They <u>roasted or grilled meat over a fire</u>.

(D) They heated water <u>by dropping hot stones into it</u>.

13. (A) The Vikings <u>built wonderful ships in the 800s</u>.

(B) Their <u>ships could sail across oceans and up shallow rivers</u>.

(C) The sailing ships were <u>long and narrow</u>.

(D) The ships had at least <u>20 pairs of oars</u>.

14. Which sentence has a compound subject?

(A) Bicycle motocross races are popular in the United States.

(B) Europeans and Australians enjoy motocross races also.

(C) Most races are held on dirt trails for a set number of laps.

(D) The racers wear helmets and padded clothing.

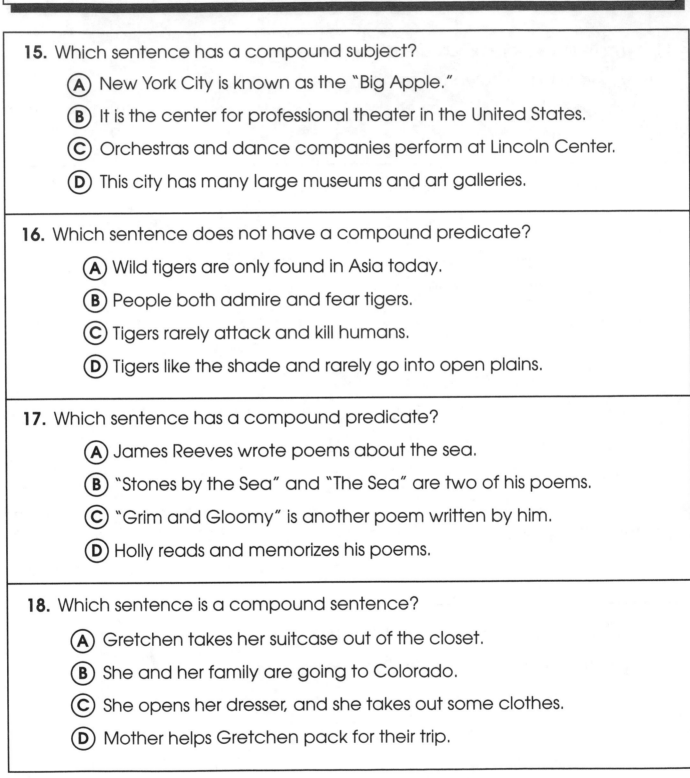

15. Which sentence has a compound subject?

   (A) New York City is known as the "Big Apple."

   (B) It is the center for professional theater in the United States.

   (C) Orchestras and dance companies perform at Lincoln Center.

   (D) This city has many large museums and art galleries.

16. Which sentence does not have a compound predicate?

   (A) Wild tigers are only found in Asia today.

   (B) People both admire and fear tigers.

   (C) Tigers rarely attack and kill humans.

   (D) Tigers like the shade and rarely go into open plains.

17. Which sentence has a compound predicate?

   (A) James Reeves wrote poems about the sea.

   (B) "Stones by the Sea" and "The Sea" are two of his poems.

   (C) "Grim and Gloomy" is another poem written by him.

   (D) Holly reads and memorizes his poems.

18. Which sentence is a compound sentence?

   (A) Gretchen takes her suitcase out of the closet.

   (B) She and her family are going to Colorado.

   (C) She opens her dresser, and she takes out some clothes.

   (D) Mother helps Gretchen pack for their trip.

GO ON

Unit 4 Test

18. Which sentence is a compound sentence?

(A) Lee hit the tennis ball hard.

(B) The serve sailed over the net.

(C) Jose quickly returned the ball, and Lee smashed it into the far court.

(D) Lee won the point and the game.

20. In which sentence are the words in the correct order?

(A) Most clothes wore Egyptians made from ancient linen.

(B) Most ancient Egyptians wore clothes made from linen.

(C) Linen clothes made from ancient Egyptians wore most.

(D) Ancient linen clothes made Egyptians most wore from.

Write a sentence with a compound predicate. Tell how it differs from a compound sentence.

_____

_____

_____

_____

59

Midway Review Test Name Grid

Write your name in pencil in the boxes along the top. Begin with your last name. Fill in as many letters as will fit. Then follow the columns straight down and bubble in the letters that correspond with the letters in your name. Complete the rest of the information the same way. You may use a piece of scrap paper to help you keep your place.

STUDENT'S NAME	SCHOOL

LAST — FIRST — MI

SCHOOL

TEACHER

FEMALE ○   MALE ○

DATE OF BIRTH

MONTH	DAY	YEAR

The name grid columns each contain bubbles: ○ A B C D E F G H I J K L M N O P Q R S T U V W X Y Z

MONTH	DAY	YEAR
JAN ○	⓪ ⓪	⓪ ⓪
FEB ○	① ①	① ①
MAR ○	② ②	② ②
APR ○	③ ③	③ ③
MAY ○	④	④ ④
JUN ○	⑤	⑤ ⑤
JUL ○	⑥	⑥ ⑥
AUG ○	⑦	⑦ ⑦
SEP ○	⑧	⑧ ⑧
OCT ○	⑨	⑨ ⑨
NOV ○		
DEC ○		

GRADE ③ ④ ⑤

Midway Review Test Answer Sheet

Pay close attention when transferring your answers. Fill in the bubbles neatly and completely. You may use a piece of scrap paper to help you keep your place.

SAMPLES
A ⒶⒷ⊙Ⓓ
B ⒻⒼ⊙ⒽⒿ

1 ⒶⒷⒸⒹ
2 ⒻⒼⒽⒿ
3 ⒶⒷⒸⒹ
4 ⒻⒼⒽⒿ
5 ⒶⒷⒸⒹ
6 ⒻⒼⒽⒿ

7 ⒶⒷⒸⒹ
8 ⒻⒼⒽⒿ
9 ⒶⒷⒸⒹ
10 ⒻⒼⒽⒿ
11 ⒶⒷⒸⒹ
12 ⒻⒼⒽⒿ

13 ⒶⒷⒸⒹ
14 ⒻⒼⒽⒿ
15 ⒶⒷⒸⒹ
16 ⒻⒼⒽⒿ
17 ⒶⒷⒸⒹ
18 ⒻⒼⒽⒿ

19 ⒶⒷⒸⒹ
20 ⒻⒼⒽⒿ

Read or listen to the directions. Fill in the circle beside the best answer.

☐ Example:

Which sentence does not have a plural noun in the subject?

(A) Many lions live in zoos.

(B) A trained lion may perform in a circus.

(C) The lions can begin their training when they are two years old.

(D) Some countries protect lions in national parks.

Answer: B because "A trained lion" is the subject. It tells what the sentence is about. "Lion" is a singular noun.

Now try these. You have 20 minutes. Continue until you see ⬡STOP .

Remember your Helping Hand Strategies:

1. Sometimes the correct answer is not given. Fill in the circle beside NG if no answer is correct.

2. Always read each question carefully.

3. Read all the answer choices before you choose the one you think is correct.

4. Fill in the answer circles completely and neatly.

---

1. What are the common nouns in the following sentence?

   Lions and tigers are the largest wild cats.

   (A) lions, tigers, largest   (B) lions, tigers, wild

   (C) lions, tigers, cats   (D) tigers, wild, cats

---

2. Which sentence does not include a proper noun?

   (F) Lions once roamed Europe and the Middle East.

   (G) Now there are only a few lions left.

   (H) Lions still live in parts of Africa.

   (J) About 200 lions live in the Gir Forest in India.

GO ON ⟩

3. Which word is a singular noun?

authors   reporter   poets   writers
(A)   (B)   (C)   (D)

4. Which is the correct plural form of **woman**?

womans   woman's   women   womens
(F)   (G)   (H)   (J)

5. Which is the correct possessive form of **child**?

children   childs   children's   child's
(A)   (B)   (C)   (D)

6. Choose the correct pronoun for the underlined words.

<u>Alpine skiing and Nordic skiing</u> are two types of skiing.

It   They   Them   His
(F)   (G)   (H)   (J)

7. Choose the correct possessive pronoun for the underlined words.

<u>My favorite ski resort</u> is in Switzerland.

Mine   It   Theirs   Your
(A)   (B)   (C)   (D)

8. What is the action verb in the sentence?

The volcano erupted suddenly on the island.

volcano   erupted   suddenly   island
(F)   (G)   (H)   (J)

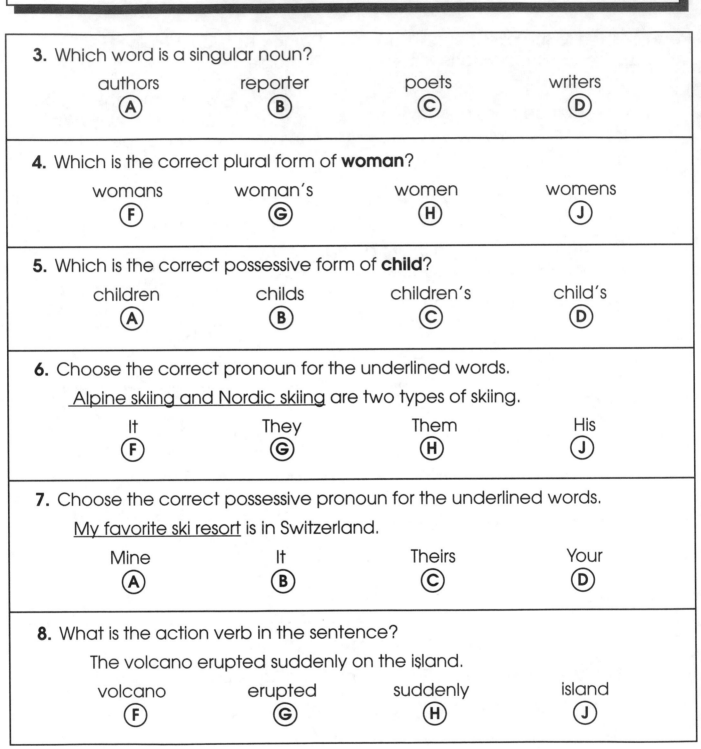

GO ON →

9. Which sentence has a helping verb?

(A) Plates are rigid sections of rock.

(B) Most volcanoes are formed where two of the earth's plates collide.

(C) The collision forces one plate under the other.

(D) Friction and heat cause it to melt.

10. Which is the correct contraction of **will not**?

wouldn't
(F)

willn't
(G)

won't
(H)

wo'nt
(J)

11. Which word is an adjective in the following sentence?

The busy beavers built a lodge yesterday.

busy
(A)

built
(B)

lodge
(C)

yesterday
(D)

12. Which word is a proper adjective in the following sentence?

Bret plays baseball for the Alaskan Huskies in Juneau.

Bret
(F)

Alaskan
(G)

Huskies
(H)

Juneau
(J)

13. Choose the correct adjective to complete the sentence.

The Huskies is a _____ team than the Malamutes.

powerfully
(A)

most powerful
(B)

powerful
(C)

more powerful
(D)

14. Which sentence does not use an article correctly?

(F) Joshua plays a clarinet.

(G) He used to play the trumpet.

(H) Someday he may want to play a oboe.

(J) His mother hopes he will not play the drums.

15. Identify the adverb in the following sentence.

Sunshine always makes me happy.

Sunshine	always	makes	happy
(A)	(B)	(C)	(D)

16. Choose the correct adverb to complete the sentence.

Sergio felt the ____ right before the game began.

anxious	more anxious	anxiously	most anxious
(F)	(G)	(H)	(J)

17. Which sentence is an interrogative sentence?

(A) I can't wait until Saturday!

(B) My family and I are going whitewater rafting.

(C) Do you think you can come with us?

(D) Please ask your parents.

18. Identify the underlined word in the following sentence.

The medic <u>rushed</u> to the aid of the accident victim.

(F) simple predicate   (G) complete subject

(H) simple subject   (J) complete predicate

GO ON

Name

19. Which sentence has a compound subject?

    (A) The sun supplies Earth with heat and light.

    (B) The sun is closer to Earth than any other star.

    (C) The sun and most stars are made of gas and plasma.

    (D) Stars are grouped in galaxies.

20. Which sentence is a compound sentence?

    (F) The sun is in the Milky Way Galaxy.

    (G) The Milky Way Galaxy contains more than 100 billion stars!

    (H) There are more than 100 billion galaxies in the universe.

    (J) The Milky Way Galaxy has many planets, and it contains more than 100 billion stars.

Does the following sentence have a compound subject or a compound predicate? Or is it a compound sentence? Write your answer and give a reason for your choice.

Michelle went to the hockey game with her father, and they had a great time together.

_____

_____

_____

_____

First word of a sentence, quotation, and I
Unit 5

The **first word** of a sentence and a quotation begin with a capital letter. The pronoun I is always a capital letter.

Example: "I would like to know how astronauts dress when they walk in space," said Monroe. (I is the first word of a sentence, the first word of a quotation, and the pronoun I.)

Fashions of the Astronauts

Read each sentence. Write **yes** if the sentence has the correct capitalization. Write **no** if it does not.

_____ 1. "Astronauts wear special suits when they walk in space," said Monroe's teacher.

_____ 2. "Their suits keep them from getting too cold or too hot."

_____ 3. "i wonder how they breathe," said Monroe.

_____ 4. Ms. Hill answered, "Their backpacks have enough air for eight hours."

_____ 5. Ms. Hill continued, "their helmets are special, too."

_____ 6. "They are equipped with microphones and headphones."

_____ 7. "A camera is attached to each helmet," she said.

Use the proofreading mark to show where each capital letter is needed.

$\underline{\underline{\text{they}}}$ went home.

8. "what do astronauts wear inside the Space Station?" asked Monroe.

9. "they do not have to wear their space suits," said Ms. Hill.

10. "i wonder why not."

11. "there's air inside the station, so they do not need to wear them."

Rewrite each sentence on another sheet of paper. Use capital letters where they are needed.

12. "they wear comfortable clothes so they can exercise," explained Ms. Hill.

13. Monroe asked, "why do they have to exercise?"

14. "since there is so little gravity in space, the astronauts just float around."

15. "their muscles and bones would get weak if they did not exercise."

Name

Names of persons and family members   Unit 5

The **first**, **middle**, and **last** names of persons begin with capital letters. Example: <u>A</u>my <u>L</u>ee <u>D</u>avis

Names of **family members** begin with capital letters when they are used as proper nouns.
Examples: <u>G</u>randfather, <u>A</u>unt <u>E</u>lsa, <u>U</u>ncle <u>I</u>ke (Note: Do not capitalize them when they are used
as common nouns, such as my grandfather, his aunt, her uncle.)

A Capital Idea

Write **yes** if each name of a person or family member is
written correctly. Write **no** if it is not.

_____ 1. eric Roberts   _____ 2. Stacey Ware

_____ 3. Grandma ruth   _____ 4. Aunt Kamella

_____ 5. Uncle Steve   _____ 6. Jerry Joe Johns

_____ 7. Ola mae Hood   _____ 8. Grandpa Jim

Write each name of a person or family member correctly.

9. cousin sylvia   10. uncle vernon

_____   _____

11. jerry andrews   12. aunt martha

_____   _____

13. paulo jo rollo   14. grandfather murray

_____   _____

Fill in the circle under each name that should begin
with a capital letter.

15. My cousin's names are grace, sylvester, and lela.
    Ⓐ   Ⓑ   Ⓒ   Ⓓ

16. They are uncle roy and aunt jan's children.
    Ⓐ   Ⓑ   Ⓒ   Ⓓ

17. My dad is their uncle, and my mother is their aunt.
    Ⓐ   Ⓑ   Ⓒ   Ⓓ

Name

Titles of respect and initials   Unit 5

Titles of respect, such as Mr., Mrs., Ms., Miss, Dr., and Rev., begin with capital letters.
They are used in front of the person's name. Example: <u>Rev.</u> Smith is our minister.

An **initial** can take the place of a person's first or middle name. It is always a capital letter.
Example: Mr. Thomas Alan Baxter becomes Mr. <u>T</u>. <u>A</u>. Baxter

V.I.P.'s

Write each name correctly. Remember that a person's
first, middle, and last names begin with capital letters.

1. mr. and mrs. foster

   _____

2. ms. maxine marshall

   _____

3. dr. c. l. smith

   _____

4. miss tiffany tyler

   _____

Write each sentence correctly.

5. mr. g. w. abbott is my violin teacher.

   _____

6. My soccer coach is paul w. young.

   _____

7. dr. julia fister is my dentist.

   _____

 Use titles of respect and initials correctly to write the names of two of
your teachers.

_____

Names of places (streets, cities, states)   Unit 5

Names of streets begin with capital letters. Sometimes they are written in a shorter way, but they still begin with capital letters. There may be more than one word in the name. Examples: <u>W</u>ellington <u>W</u>ay, <u>C</u>astle <u>Dr</u>., <u>S</u>pring <u>C</u>reek <u>C</u>t.

Names of cities and states begin with capital letters. There may be more than one word in the name. **Two-letter postal abbreviations** for states are capitalized. Examples: <u>R</u>ichland, <u>M</u>ichigan; <u>W</u>hiting, <u>NJ</u>

This Must Be the Place

Write each sentence correctly.

1. Mrs. Wolf lived in perryville, tn, and oceanside, ca.

   _____

2. Terri rode her bike from ninth street to echo hill drive.

   _____

3. jupiter island, florida, is where my grandparents live.

   _____

4. my aunt and uncle went to college in iowa city, ia.

   _____

5. Carter and his family drove to 927 jenkins lane in pond, mississippi.

   _____

6. My Uncle Dwayne lives on sunset drive in bartlesville, oklahoma.

   _____

7. Do you know if Connie lives on sunshine drive or ridge rd.?

   _____

8. Mr. Hall's address is 1616 white oaks ave.

   _____

9. Mary moved from platte city, missouri, to lincoln, nebraska.

   _____

Name

Names of things (days, months, holidays, special days, and their abbreviations)

Names of days of the week and months of the year begin with capital letters.
Abbreviations of days and months begin with capital letters.
Examples: Sunday/Sun., January/Jan.

Names of special days and holidays begin with capital letters.
Examples: Independence Day, Arbor Day

What Is the Date?

Write each sentence correctly.

1. Basketball practices are on thursdays and saturdays.

   _____

2. Seth is having friends spend the night on wednesday for new year's eve.

   _____

   _____

3. Laura's surprise party is friday, february 5.

   _____

4. My family celebrates mother's day and thanksgiving day at my aunt's house.

   _____

   _____

5. This year labor day is monday, september 3.

   _____

6. Carole's birthday is next saturday, march 12.

   _____

7. christmas eve is always december 24.

   _____

8. presidents' day is celebrated on the third monday in february.

   _____

Name

Proper adjectives and proper nouns

A **proper noun** names a **special person**, **place**, or **thing**. It begins with a capital letter.
Examples: Paul, Boston, Congress

A **proper adjective** is a proper noun used as an adjective. It begins with a capital letter.
Example: Boston/the Boston Commons

A **proper adjective** may be formed by adding an ending to a proper noun. It begins with a capital letter. Example: America/American soldiers

The War of Independence

Identify the underlined word or words as a proper adjective or proper noun. Write **PA** for proper adjective or **PN** for proper noun above the underlined word or words.

1. The <u>American</u> Revolution began in 1775.

2. <u>Minutemen</u> and <u>British</u> redcoats fought at <u>Lexington</u> and <u>Concord</u>.

3. <u>George Washington</u> was the leader of the <u>Continental</u> Army.

4. The <u>British</u> won the <u>Battle of Bunker Hill</u>.

5. On <u>July</u> 4, 1776, the <u>Congress</u> adopted the <u>Declaration of Independence</u>.

Rewrite each sentence below on another sheet of paper. Use capital letters for proper nouns and proper adjectives.

6. british troops occupied new york city in september, 1776.

7. general washington led the americans to several victories in 1777.

8. The british also won some battles, and they occupied philadelphia.

9. Then in 1778, france came to the aid of the united states.

10. cornwallis surrendered to the americans at yorktown in 1781.

11. great britain and the united states signed a peace treaty on september 3, 1783.

Friendly letters and business letters

Friendly letters and **business letters** differ in their purposes, but the same capitalization rules apply to both types of letters. In addition to the five parts of a friendly letter—the heading, the greeting, the body of the letter, the closing, and the name—a business letter has an inside address and a signature.

The first word and proper nouns in the greeting begin with capital letters.
Example of a greeting for a friendly letter: <u>D</u>ear <u>M</u>om and <u>D</u>ad,
Example of a greeting for a business letter: <u>D</u>ear <u>T</u>oy <u>P</u>alace:

The first word of the closing begins with a capital letter.
Example of a closing for a friendly and a business letter: <u>S</u>incerely yours,

Special Delivery

Use the proofreading mark to show where each capital letter is needed in the friendly letter.

1819 primrose lane
bend, oregon 97701
august 1, 2001

dear barbara,

    i am really enjoying my summer vacation here on my uncle's ranch. there are horses to ride and my cousins and i go fishing. i'll see you in two more weeks, and then i can show you my pictures.

your friend,

bonnie

Use the proofreading mark to show where each capital letter is needed in the business letter.

4407 ninth street
hillside, maine 04024
march 10, 2000

mr. john jones
skateboards and more
6243 rock ave.
detroit, michigan 48201

dear mr. jones:

    i am returning my skateboard for repair. it is still under warranty. please repair it, and return the skateboard to the address above as soon as possible.

sincerely,

sam smith

sam smith

Name

Outline form

An **outline** is an excellent tool to use for writing a **report**. It contains information taken from notes made about the subject of the report.

The first word, the last word, and the important words in the title and each main idea begin with capital letters. The first word of each supporting detail begins with a capital letter.

Study the example of an outline below. Notice the use of Roman numerals for main ideas and capital letters for supporting details.

Writing an Outline

Table Tennis

I. Definition of Table Tennis
  A. Indoor game
  B. Similar to tennis
  C. Also called Ping-Pong

II. Equipment for Table Tennis
  A. Table 9 feet long, 5 feet wide, 30 inches high
  B. Net across width at center of table 6 inches high
  C. Rackets made of wood covered with ⅙ inch sponge
  D. Round, hollow, celluloid ball weighs ¹⁄₁₁ ounce

III. How Singles Game Is Played
  A. Ball hit over net with racket
  B. Must return ball after one bounce
  C. Ball to clear the net and bounce once on opponent's court
  D. Point scored if bad serve or return
  E. Serve changed after every five points
  F. Winning score 21 points, with a 2-point lead

Use the proofreading mark to show where each capital letter is needed in the outline below.

abacus

I. history of the abacus

  a. ancient device used to calculate mathematical problems

  b. used by early Greeks, Romans, and Chinese

II. the abacus

  a. frame with columns of beads

  b. beads strung on wires or rods

  c. two beads on every column above a crossbar and 5 beads below

  d. numbers shown by moving the appropriate beads to crossbar

Name

Book and magazine titles

Begin the first word, the last word, and each important word in the **title of a book or magazine** with a capital letter. Examples: <u>A</u>rrow to the <u>S</u>un (*arrow* is the first word of the book title. *Sun* is the last word. *To* and *the* are not important words in the title and should not be capitalized unless they are the first words.)

Underline the title of a book or magazine when it is in a sentence.
Example: <u>Boy's Life</u> is a magazine title.

Let's Go to the Library

Write each book or magazine title correctly.

1. sukey and the mermaid

   _____

2. kids discover

   _____

3. nowhere to call home

   _____

4. dave at night

   _____

5. speed of light

   _____

6. heart of a tiger

   _____

Write each sentence correctly. Remember to underline book and magazine titles in sentences.

7. Tara read julie of the wolves by Jean Craighead.

   _____

8. John said the view from saturday is a good book.

   _____

9. Did Karen Hess write out of the dust?

   _____

10. Jamar enjoys reading u.s. kids.

    _____

11. Joe's favorite magazine is national geographic world.

    _____

Name

Stories, articles, poems, and songs

Begin the first word, the last word, and each important word in the **titles of stories**, **articles** from newspapers and magazines, **poems**, and **songs** with capital letters. Quotation marks are used around these titles.

Examples: "Who Rules the Roost?" (story), "The Eyes Have It" (article), "Autumn Woods" (poem), "Put on a Happy Face" (song)

Time for Titles

Write each title correctly.

1. "loveliest of trees"

   _____

2. "home on the range"

   _____

3. "if i were a bell"

   _____

4. "the fisherman and his wife"

   _____

Use the proofreading mark to show where each capital letter is needed in titles of stories, articles, poems, and songs.

5. Robert Frost wrote a poem called "the runaway."

6. "hummingbird imposters" is an article about moths that behave like hummingbirds.

7. "this is my country" is a patriotic song.

8. Carl Sandburg's "primer lesson" is a thoughtful poem.

9. "diving for doubloons" is a fascinating article.

10. "mother to son" is a poem by Langston Hughes.

Write the titles of two of your favorite stories or songs on another sheet of paper.

Unit 5 Test

Mechanics: Capitalization

Read or listen to the directions. Fill in the circle beside the best answer.

❑ Example:

Which word or words should not begin with capital letters?

(A) Stanley   (B) Uncle Jerry

(C) Aunt   (D) Frank P. Lee

Cross out answers you know are wrong.

Answer: C because **aunt** is not a proper noun.

Now try these. You have 20 minutes. Continue until you see ⬡STOP.

---

1. Which sentence is written correctly?

(A) Last week mother and i went to the zoo.

(B) Mom and i saw a new insect exhibit.

(C) I thought the tarantulas were neat.

(D) We also saw several Walking sticks.

---

2. Which quotation is not written correctly?

(A) "where were you born?" asked Marilou.

(B) "I was born in Buffalo, New York," I answered.

(C) "Oh, I have an aunt who lives in Buffalo," Marilou said.

(D) "How long has she lived there?" I asked.

---

3. Which name is not written correctly?

Grandpa Joe	Billy rider	James Young	Cam L. Trapp
(A)	(B)	(C)	(D)

GO ON ➤

Name

4. Which title of respect and name is written correctly?

(A) Mr. Tom Tucker   (B) Ms. Natalie comer

(C) Dr. Pauline painter   (D) Gen. Stuart t. Latta

5. Which street name is not written correctly?

(A) Anthony Lane   (B) Ridgefield Ave.

(C) Pretty Valley Dr.   (D) Parker rd.

6. Which city and state is written correctly?

(A) Lawton, ok   (B) Belle Center, Missouri

(C) Partridge, kentucky   (D) Newport beach, CA

7. Which sentence is not written correctly?

(A) Tara's birthday is next Monday.

(B) Is that on September 4?

(C) It is the same day as labor day.

(D) Will she have her party on Saturday?

8. Which sentence is written correctly?

(A) John is a native alaskan.

(B) He lives in Anchorage.

(C) The state of alaska is our largest state.

(D) The capital of Alaska is juneau.

GO ON

Unit 5 Test

9. Which line of the friendly letter heading is not correct?

7708 Hilltop lane
Ⓐ

Atlanta, Georgia 30301
Ⓑ

March 10, 2000
Ⓒ

10. Which greeting of a friendly letter is written correctly?

Ⓐ Dear Mr. And Mrs. Reed,

Ⓑ Dear Tad and tom,

Ⓒ Dear Helen,

Ⓓ NG

11. Choose the closing that is not written correctly.

Your Friend,
Ⓐ

Sincerely yours,
Ⓑ

Sincerely,
Ⓒ

Yours truly,
Ⓓ

12. Which supporting detail in an outline is not written correctly?

Ⓐ A. Different sizes of stars

Ⓑ B. Different colors of stars

Ⓒ C. Stars' Different Brightness Levels

Ⓓ   D. Names of stars

13. Which book title is written correctly?

Ⓐ Henry And Mudge

Ⓑ The Day It snowed Tortillas

Ⓒ The Cat ate my Gymsuit

Ⓓ Golem and the Dragon Girl

14. Which story title is written correctly?

Ⓐ The Talking pot

Ⓑ "The talking Pot"

Ⓒ The Talking Pot

Ⓓ NG

GO ON

78

15. Choose the sentence with the book title that is written correctly.

  (A) Jess read <u>Mirandy and Brother Wind</u>.

  (B) Jess read "Mirandy and Brother Wind."

  (C) Jess read <u>Mirandy And Brother Wind</u>.

  (D) Jess read "Mirandy and brother Wind."

16. Which sentence is written correctly?

  (A) Your big Backyard is a magazine about nature.

  (B) Yolanda enjoys reading "your big backyard."

  (C) She reads <u>Your Big Backyard</u> at the library.

  (D) She learns many interesting things in "Your Big Backyard."

17. Which sentence is written correctly?

  (A) <u>American Heartbreak</u> is a poem by Langston Hughes.

  (B) american heartbreak is a poem by Langston Hughes.

  (C) "American Heartbreak" is a poem by Langston Hughes.

  (D) "American heartbreak" is a poem by Langston Hughes.

18. Which song title is written correctly?

  (A) What a Wonderful World

  (B) "What a wonderful World"

  (C) "What A Wonderful World"

  (D) "What a Wonderful World"

19. Which title of an article is written correctly?

(A) "life in the ocean of air"

(B) Life in the ocean of Air

(C) "Life in the Ocean of Air"

(D) <u>Life in the ocean of air</u>

20. Which sentence is written correctly?

(A) Mark and penny went to the City Library.

(B) Mark checked out the book, "Soccer, Jr."

(C) Penny selected American Girl.

(D) Penny is going to check out <u>Highlights</u> next time.

Read the following sentence. Explain the use of each capital in the sentence.

Mrs. Madison gave Kate the magazine titled <u>Girl's Life</u>.

_____

_____

_____

Name

Periods for declarative, imperative, and compound sentences   Unit 6

A **declarative sentence** tells a complete idea. It ends with a **period** (.).
Example: A male swan is called a cob.

An **imperative sentence** gives an order. It ends with a **period** (.).
Example: Tell me what a female swan is called.

A **compound sentence** combines two sentences. It ends with a **period** (.).
Example: Swans have webbed feet, and they are good swimmers.

Swimming With Swans

Identify each sentence and add
a period. Write **D** for a declarative
sentence, **I** for an imperative sentence,
or **C** for a compound sentence.

_____ 1. Swans are water birds related
to ducks and geese

_____ 2. Most swans are larger than
ducks and geese, and they
have longer necks

_____ 3. Tell me where swans live

_____ 4. They live on all continents except Africa and Antarctica

_____ 5. Name some different species of swans

_____ 6. Mute, tundra, whooper, and trumpeter swans live north of the equator

_____ 7. Black, black-necked, and Coscoroba swans live south of the equator

_____ 8. Swans feed on underwater plants, and they eat grasses along the shore

_____ 9. Swans usually mate for life, and they build large nests

_____ 10. The female swan lays four to six eggs in the nest

Write each sentence correctly on another sheet of paper.

11. Swan eggs must be kept warm until they hatch

12. Baby swans are called cygnets

13. Cygnets cannot fly for almost two months

14. They may ride on their parents' backs

Periods for titles of respect, initials, and abbreviations — Unit 6

Use a **period** after a **title of respect**, such as Mr., Mrs., Ms., Dr., and Rev. (but not after Miss). Examples: Mrs. Hatton, Mr. Temple

Use a **period** after an **initial**. Examples: T. R. Young, Brenda F. Kramer

Use a **period** after an **abbreviation**. (Do not use a period with a two-letter postal abbreviation such as KS or CA.) Examples: Sunday/Sun., Street/St.

Powerful Punctuation!

Write each name correctly.

1. Mr Carl L Dyer

   _____

2. Mr and Mrs W W Davis

   _____

3. Rev and Mrs Pogue

   _____

4. Ms Janetta Lewis

   _____

5. Dr Greg T Ward

   _____

6. Miss Rita R Reynolds

   _____

Write the correct abbreviation for each word.

7. Monday _____   8. Lane _____

9. April _____   10. Friday _____

11. Road _____   12. Saturday _____

13. Court _____   14. Avenue _____

Use the proofreading mark to show where each period should be added in the note below.

> To show where a period is needed, add the period in the correct place and circle it. ⊙

Date: Feb 1, 2001

To: Mrs Cora K Kramer

From: Miss Mitchell

The date of your school conference about Tommy has been changed to Tues, Mar 6, at the same time. I hope this time is convenient for you.

Name

Periods in outline form

When writing an **outline**, use **periods after Roman numerals** for main ideas. Use **periods after capital letters** for supporting details.

Outlines for Astronauts

Study the example of an outline below.

Sally Ride

I. Early Life
   A. Born in Los Angeles
   B. Ph.D. degree in physics from Stanford University
   C. Became an astronaut

II. Achievements as an Astronaut
   A. First American woman to travel in space
   B. Made a 6-day flight on the *Challenger* space shuttle in 1983
   C. Used shuttle's remote manipulator arm
   D. Made second shuttle flight in 1984

III. Later Life
   A. Resigned astronaut program in 1987
   B. Became professor of physics at University of California at San Diego in 1989
   C. Served as director of the California Space Institute

Use the proofreading mark to show where each period is needed in the outline below.

John Glenn, Jr.

I Early Life

   A Born July 18, 1921, in Cambridge, Ohio

   B Grew up in New Concord, Ohio

II Military Service

   A Became World War II Marine Corps pilot

   B Flew combat missions during the Korean War

   C Earned 5 Distinguished Flying Crosses and 19 Air Medals

III Years as an Astronaut

   A Chosen as one of the original *Mercury* astronauts in 1959

   B First American to orbit Earth on Feb. 20, 1962

   C *Friendship 7* flight lasted 4 hours 55 minutes

Question marks and exclamation marks   Unit 6

An **interrogative sentence** asks a question. Use a **question mark** (**?**) at the end of the sentence. Example: Did you know that some dolphins have 252 teeth?

An **exclamatory sentence** shows great emotion. Use an **exclamation mark** (**!**) at the end of an exclamatory sentence. An exclamatory sentence often begins or ends with an interjection such as *wow*. Example: Wow, that is a lot of teeth!

Talking About Teeth

Put a question mark at the end of each interrogative sentence. Put an exclamation mark at the end of each exclamatory sentence.

1. Do you know how many teeth an adult human has

2. Does he or she have 32 teeth

3. Did you realize that zebras have teeth like rats

4. Hey, you must be kidding

5. Wow, zebras grind down their teeth by eating 15 hours a day

6. Can their teeth just keep growing like rodents' teeth

7. That is amazing

8. Is it true that great white sharks have razor-sharp teeth

Rewrite each sentence. Add the correct ending mark.

9. You will not believe this

_____

10. What are you talking about

_____

11. Wow, a snail has teeth on its tongue

_____

12. Goodness, there are thousands of tiny teeth

_____

Name

Commas in dates, cities and states, and in letters

Use a **comma** (,) to separate the **day** from the **year**. Example: August 6, 1995

Also use a **comma** after the **year** if it is not the last word in a sentence.
Example: August 6, 1995, was the date on which Julia was born.

Use a **comma** to separate the name of a **city** from the **state**. Example: Toledo, Ohio

Also use a **comma** after the name of the **state** if it is not the last word in a sentence.
Example: Toledo, Ohio, was Julia's birthplace.

Use a **comma** after the **greeting** of a friendly letter and after the **closing** of both a friendly letter and a business letter. Examples: Dear Julia, (greeting)   Sincerely, (closing)

Commas, Commas, Commas!

Write each date, city and state, greeting, or closing correctly.

1. Spring Grove Minnesota

_____

2. Dear Gramps

_____

3. Your cousin

_____

4. October 9 2001

_____

5. North Branch New York

_____

6. Dear Uncle Gerald

_____

7. March 3 2001

_____

8. Fall Leaf KS

_____

Use the proofreading mark to show where each comma is needed in the friendly letter below.

> To show where a comma is needed, add the comma with an insert direction. ⌄

9220 Peachtree Lane

Ocean View California

October 15 2001

Dear Josie and Ted

   I will be arriving on the 3:00 P.M. train from Reno Nevada on October 25.
I hope you can meet me at the station in Barstow California at that time.

Your friend
Martina

Name

Commas in series

Use **commas** (,) to **separate a series** of three or more things or actions in a sentence. Use *and* before the last noun or verb. Examples: Mary, Ann, Ray, *and* Rob went on a trip with their parents. (In this example, there are four children going on a trip.)

The correct use of commas is important to the meaning of a sentence. Example: Mary Ann, Ray, *and* Rob went on a trip with their parents. (In this example, three children are named.)

Trip Time!

Are the commas used correctly in each sentence? Write **yes** or **no** on the blank.

_____ 1. The Smiths visited Philadelphia, and New, York.

_____ 2. They saw museums, of art, history and science in Philadelphia.

_____ 3. Don, Debbie, and Dan toured Independence Hall.

_____ 4. The Declaration of Independence, and the Constitution were signed there.

_____ 5. The Smiths saw the Betsy Ross House, Christ Church, and the United States Mint.

In the sentences below, use the proofreading mark to show where each comma is needed.

6. Debbie Don and Dan were impressed with New York City.

7. It is an important business cultural and trade center.

8. The Bronx Manhattan Queens Brooklyn and Staten Island are its five boroughs.

9. Chinatown Greenwich Village and Harlem are three neighborhoods in Manhattan.

10. The Smiths saw Times Square Rockefeller Center and the United Nations Headquarters.

11. Central Park surprised them with its grass trees lakes and hills in the heart of the city.

12. New York City has many concert halls theaters and museums.

13. The Smiths visited the Metropolitan Museum of Art the Guggenheim Museum and the American Museum of Natural History.

Name

Commas in direct addresses, appositives, and compound sentences   Unit 6

Use a **comma** (,) to set apart the name of the person being spoken to directly from the rest of the sentence. Examples: Kim, do you know falcons are birds of prey? Where can I learn more about falcons, Alex?

Use **commas** to separate an appositive that immediately follows a noun from the rest of the sentence. An **appositive** is a word or phrase that explains or identifies a noun. Examples: Falcons, *birds of prey*, live on high, rocky cliffs. (The phrase *birds of prey* identifies the noun *falcons*. Without the phrase, a reader may not know that falcons are birds of prey.) Some birds of prey, *like falcons*, live on high, rocky cliffs. (The phrase *like falcons* identifies one kind of bird of prey.)

Use a **comma** to separate the two parts of a **compound sentence**. Example: There are about 40 species of falcons, and half the species are found in Africa.

Falcons, Birds of Prey

Use the proofreading mark to show where each comma is needed in the sentences.

1. Kim let's look at this book about falcons.

2. Falcons like hawks have hooked beaks and feet with claws.

3. Falcons are powerful fliers and they can swoop from great heights.

4. The American kestrel the smallest North American falcon is only 8 inches long.

5. A bird of prey the American kestrel eats insects, mice, lizards, and other birds.

6. Peregrine falcons amazing fliers can reach speeds of 200 miles per hour.

7. What do peregrines prefer to eat Alex?

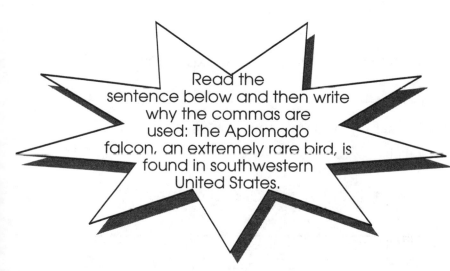

Read the sentence below and then write why the commas are used: The Aplomado falcon, an extremely rare bird, is found in southwestern United States.

8. They eat birds and that is why they are sometimes called duck hawks.

9. The gyrfalcon the largest species of falcon is 2 feet long.

10. Gyrfalcons live in Arctic regions Kim.

Name

When two or more people are talking, they are having a conversation. A **dialogue** is the conversation in written form. Use **quotation marks** (" ") around the spoken words.

The speaker's tag tells who is speaking. Use a **comma** (,) after the speaker's tag when it begins a sentence.

Example: Cory asked, "What are you reading?"
          (speaker' tag)   (dialogue)

Use a comma after the spoken words and before the **quotation marks** (" ") when the speaker's tag is at the end of a sentence.

Example: "I'm reading a story about Nadia Comaneci," answered Cassie.
                    (dialogue)   (speaker's tag)

The Perfect Gymnast

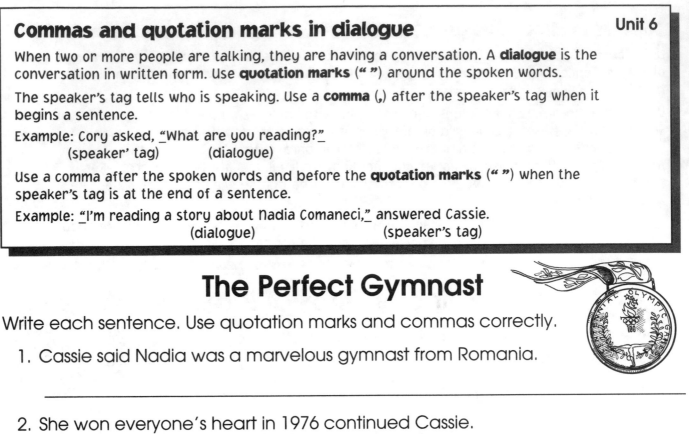

Write each sentence. Use quotation marks and commas correctly.

1. Cassie said Nadia was a marvelous gymnast from Romania.

_____

2. She won everyone's heart in 1976 continued Cassie.

_____

3. Cory asked What happened to make Nadia so popular?

_____

4. Cassie said First she won the American Cup Championship.

_____

5. She scored a perfect 10 for her vault Cassie explained.

_____

6. Cassie added Then Nadia received a 10 for her floor exercise.

_____

7. Cory asked Did she ever perform in the Olympics?

_____

8. Yes, she won three gold medals, a silver medal, and a bronze medal in 1976.

_____

_____

Name

Quotation marks in titles of stories, articles, songs, and poems   Unit 6

Use **quotation marks** around **titles of stories, articles, poems,** and **songs.**

Examples: "The Elephant's Child" (story), "Bone Collectors" (article), "Feelin' Groovy" (song), "The Falling Star" (poem)

Family Favorites

Write each story title correctly.

1. Master of All Masters

_____

2. The Golden Touch

_____

Write each title of an article correctly.

3. Hidden Hunter

_____

4. Scuba, Anyone?

_____

5. Stop the Food Fight!

_____

6. Spin Control

_____

Write each song title correctly.

7. Leader of the Pack

_____

8. Monster Mash

_____

9. Y.M.C.A.

_____

10. Castle on a Cloud

_____

Write each title of a poem correctly.

11. Hear America Singing

_____

12. Cat and the Weather

_____

13. A Modern Dragon

_____

14. Paul Revere's Ride

_____

Name _____

Apostrophes in contractions and possessive nouns Unit 6

An **apostrophe** (') is used in place of the letter or letters deleted from a **contraction**.
Many contractions are made by joining linking verbs and the word *not*.
Example: do not/<u>don't</u> (An apostrophe takes the place of the *o* in *not*.)

Some contractions are made by joining pronouns and verbs. An apostrophe (') is used
in place of the letter or letters left out. Example: I will/<u>I'll</u> (An apostrophe takes the
place of the *wi* in *will*.)

Add an **apostrophe** and **-s** ('s) to most singular common and proper nouns to show
possession. Add an apostrophe (') to most common and proper plural nouns to show
possession. Add an apostrophe and **-s** ('s) to irregular plural nouns to show possession.
Examples: the book<u>'s</u> title, the stories<u>'</u> illustrators, the people<u>'s</u> favorite poems

Let's Read!

Write the contraction for each pair of words.

1. you have _____   2. we are _____

3. he will _____   4. have not _____

5. she has _____   6. I am _____

Rewrite each phrase using a possessive noun for each underlined noun.
Example: the book of Charles <u>Dickens</u>/Charles Dickens's book

7. the stories of Rudyard <u>Kipling</u> _____

8. the tales of Hans Christian <u>Andersen</u> _____

9. the illustrations of David <u>Small</u> _____

Each of the following sentences contains a word with an apostrophe. Write **C** if
the word with the apostrophe is a contraction. Write **PN** if it is a possessive noun.

_____ 10. Daniel Defoe's book, <u>Robinson Crusoe</u>, was written in 1719.

_____ 11. It's an adventure story of a lone man stranded on a island.

_____ 12. <u>Gulliver's Travels</u> was written in 1726 by Jonathan Swift.

_____ 13. Carmella hasn't read that book yet.

_____ 14. <u>A Child's Garden of Verses</u> is a book of poems written in 1885.

_____ 15. Let's read <u>The Jungle Book</u> next.

Name

Read or listen to the directions. Fill in the circle beside the best answer.

☐ Example:

Which ending mark should be at the end of this sentence?

Give me the magazine

(A) period

(B) question mark

(C) exclamation mark

(D) comma

Use your time wisely. If a question seems too tough, skip it and come back to it later.

Answer: A because the sentence is an imperative sentence.

Now try these. You have 20 minutes. Continue until you see ⬡STOP .

1. Which sentence should not end with a period?

(A) What is an oceanographer

(B) An oceanographer is a scientist who studies the oceans

(C) Some oceanographers study the animals that live in the oceans

(D) Tell me how to become an oceanographer

2. Which name is written correctly?

(A) Mr Allen J. Fox

(B) Miss Amy Bartlett

(C) Mrs Cleo Cunningham

(D) Dr. Francis K Macy

3. Which punctuation mark is used with an abbreviation?

(A) comma

(B) period

(C) question mark

(D) NG

4. Which punctuation mark is used after a Roman numeral in an outline?

(A) exclamation point

(B) question mark

(C) comma

(D) period

5. Which sentence has the correct ending mark?

(A) An active volcano erupts constantly?

(B) A dormant volcano has become inactive?

(C) Is Mount Kenya an extinct volcano?

(D) Volcanoes are fascinating?

6. Which ending mark should be used with this sentence?

Wow, the sun is about 4.6 billion years old

(A) comma

(B) period

(C) question mark

(D) exclamation mark

7. Which date is written correctly?

(A) September 11 2000

(B) Nov 6, 2001

(C) March 17, 1999

(D) July, 25 2001

8. Which greeting of a friendly letter is not written correctly?

(A) Dear Mom and Dad,

(B) Dear Aunt Jane,

(C) Dear Albert.

(D) Dear Mr. Schmidt,

GO ON

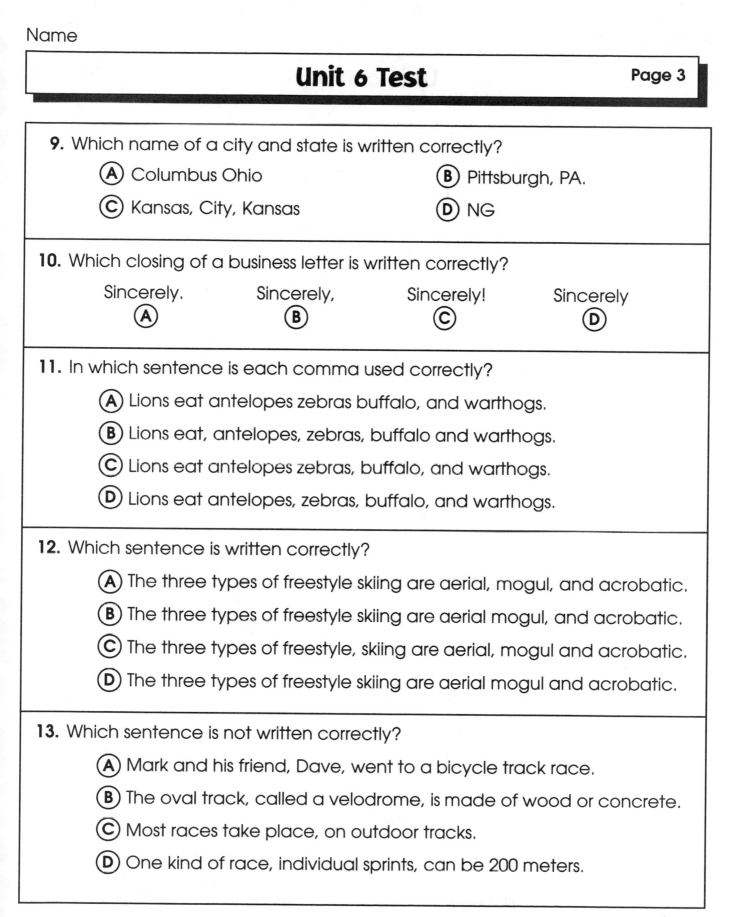

9. Which name of a city and state is written correctly?

   (A) Columbus Ohio   (B) Pittsburgh, PA.

   (C) Kansas, City, Kansas   (D) NG

10. Which closing of a business letter is written correctly?

    Sincerely.   Sincerely,   Sincerely!   Sincerely
    (A)   (B)   (C)   (D)

11. In which sentence is each comma used correctly?

    (A) Lions eat antelopes zebras buffalo, and warthogs.

    (B) Lions eat, antelopes, zebras, buffalo and warthogs.

    (C) Lions eat antelopes zebras, buffalo, and warthogs.

    (D) Lions eat antelopes, zebras, buffalo, and warthogs.

12. Which sentence is written correctly?

    (A) The three types of freestyle skiing are aerial, mogul, and acrobatic.

    (B) The three types of freestyle skiing are aerial mogul, and acrobatic.

    (C) The three types of freestyle, skiing are aerial, mogul and acrobatic.

    (D) The three types of freestyle skiing are aerial mogul and acrobatic.

13. Which sentence is not written correctly?

    (A) Mark and his friend, Dave, went to a bicycle track race.

    (B) The oval track, called a velodrome, is made of wood or concrete.

    (C) Most races take place, on outdoor tracks.

    (D) One kind of race, individual sprints, can be 200 meters.

GO ON

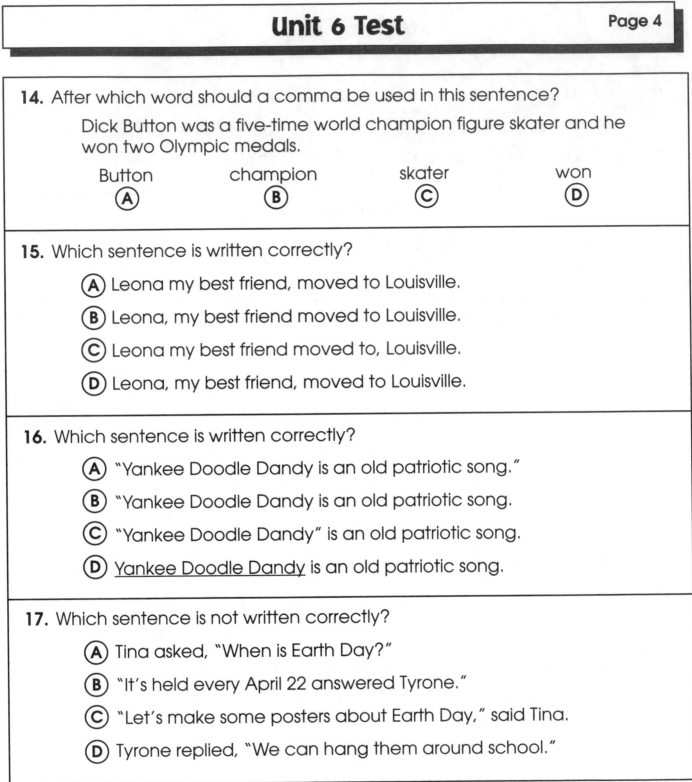

14. After which word should a comma be used in this sentence?

Dick Button was a five-time world champion figure skater and he won two Olympic medals.

Button Ⓐ   champion Ⓑ   skater Ⓒ   won Ⓓ

15. Which sentence is written correctly?

Ⓐ Leona my best friend, moved to Louisville.

Ⓑ Leona, my best friend moved to Louisville.

Ⓒ Leona my best friend moved to, Louisville.

Ⓓ Leona, my best friend, moved to Louisville.

16. Which sentence is written correctly?

Ⓐ "Yankee Doodle Dandy is an old patriotic song."

Ⓑ "Yankee Doodle Dandy is an old patriotic song.

Ⓒ "Yankee Doodle Dandy" is an old patriotic song.

Ⓓ <u>Yankee Doodle Dandy</u> is an old patriotic song.

17. Which sentence is not written correctly?

Ⓐ Tina asked, "When is Earth Day?"

Ⓑ "It's held every April 22 answered Tyrone."

Ⓒ "Let's make some posters about Earth Day," said Tina.

Ⓓ Tyrone replied, "We can hang them around school."

GO ON

18. Which punctuation mark is needed following the word **asked**?

Roberto asked "Do you know where I left my backpack?"

(A) period   (B) question mark

(C) comma   (D) exclamation point

19. Which sentence is not written correctly?

(A) Ted knows all the words to "Song of the Sky Loom."

(B) He can also recite The Wonderful World.

(C) His favorite poem is "April Rain Song" by Langston Hughes.

(D) He read "The White Knight's Song" in class.

20. In which sentence is the apostrophe not used correctly?

(A) Brandon's father is a firefighter.

(B) That's a very important job.

(C) Firefighter's rescue people from burning buildings.

(D) He's a very courageous man.

Read the two sentences below. Explain why the placement of the commas is important to the meaning of each sentence.

Carole Anne, Stacey, and Melanie ordered a pizza.

Carole, Anne, Stacey, and Melanie ordered a pizza.

_____

_____

_____

Name _____

Homophones

Homophones are words that are pronounced the same, but are spelled differently, and have different meanings. Homophones are often confusing.

Example: The <u>hair</u> of the <u>hare</u> is grayish-brown. (*Hair* and *hare* sound the same, but *hair* is the *hair* on your head, and *hare* is an animal similar to a rabbit.)

Helpful Homophones

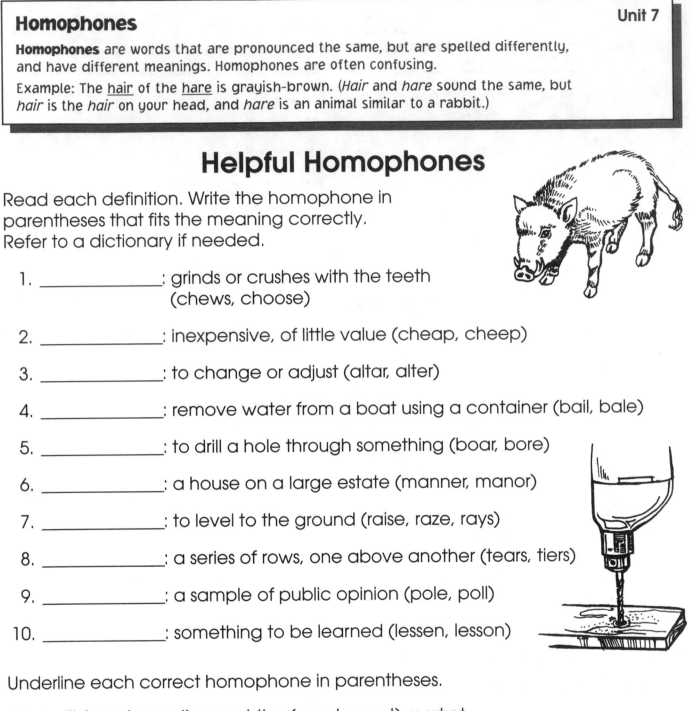

Read each definition. Write the homophone in parentheses that fits the meaning correctly. Refer to a dictionary if needed.

1. _____: grinds or crushes with the teeth (chews, choose)

2. _____: inexpensive, of little value (cheap, cheep)

3. _____: to change or adjust (altar, alter)

4. _____: remove water from a boat using a container (bail, bale)

5. _____: to drill a hole through something (boar, bore)

6. _____: a house on a large estate (manner, manor)

7. _____: to level to the ground (raise, raze, rays)

8. _____: a series of rows, one above another (tears, tiers)

9. _____: a sample of public opinion (pole, poll)

10. _____: something to be learned (lessen, lesson)

Underline each correct homophone in parentheses.

11. I will (meat, meet) you at the (meat, meet) market.

12. Joel (stairs, stares) at the number of (stairs, stares) to be climbed.

13. One (might, mite) not be able to see a (might, mite) without a microscope.

14. Kelly (peers, piers) at the many (peers, piers) in the harbor.

On another sheet of paper, write a sentence for each pair of homophones: ate, eight; one, won; knight, night; way, weigh.

Name _____

Homophones are words that are pronounced the same, but are spelled differently, and have different meanings. Homophones are often confusing. Example: The <u>prince</u> <u>prints</u> books. (*Prince* and *prints* sound the same, but *prince* is a man in a royal family and *prints* in this sentence means to publish.)

Rescue at (Sea, See)!

Complete each sentence with the correct homophone in parentheses.

1. The United States Coast Guard _____ people and ships in trouble in the water. (aides, aids)

2. The Coast Guard's lifeboats may be small _____ large. (oar, or)

3. _____ able to do different kinds of work. (Their, They're)

4. Rescuers _____ small inflatable boats close to shore. (ewes, use)

5. Large boats have powerful radios and equipment _____ navigation. (for, four)

6. They have first aid kits, survival gear, and stretchers on _____ . (board, bored)

7. The Coast Guard can _____ a disabled ship to shore. (toe, tow)

8. Rescues at _____ are often difficult. (sea, see)

9. For example, a _____ sailor is in trouble. (loan, lone)

10. The Coast Guard races to the _____ in a helicopter. (scene, seen)

11. The crew reaches the person in _____. (thyme, time)

12. A medic gives the sailor emergency care on the _____ back to shore. (way, weigh)

Choose five homophones you did not use as correct answers in the exercise above. On another sheet of paper, write a sentence for each one. Refer to a dictionary if needed.

Name

Using pronouns correctly

You and **I** are **pronouns** that can be used as the **subject** of a sentence. They can stand alone. Example: <u>You</u> and <u>I</u> are studying about famines.

He, she, it, we, and **they** are **subject pronouns** that can replace nouns and phrases containing nouns in the subject of a sentence. Example: <u>Mr. Oliver</u> showed us a video. <u>He</u> showed us a video.

An **object pronoun** is used in the predicate of a sentence. It receives the action of the verb. **You** and **me** are object pronouns that can stand alone.
Example: Mr. Oliver told <u>you</u> and <u>me</u> about famines.

Him, her, it, us, and **them** are **object pronouns** Example: Mr. Oliver read <u>our class</u> articles about famines. Mr. Oliver read <u>us</u> articles about famines.

Pronouns for You and Me

Replace the underlined word or words with the correct subject pronoun or object pronoun. Then rewrite the sentence.

1. <u>A famine</u> is a drastic wide-spread shortage of food.

   _____

2. <u>Famines</u> lead to hunger and malnutrition.

   _____

3. Disease and starvation lead to <u>many deaths</u>.

   _____

4. <u>The main cause of famines</u> is droughts.

   _____

5. <u>A drought</u> is a long period of little or no rain in an area.

   _____

6. <u>Mr. Oliver</u> said, "Then the topsoil is blown away."

   _____

7. <u>You and I</u> learned the land is not good for farming anymore.

   _____

8. Natural disasters can cause <u>famines</u>, also.

   _____

Name

Irregular verbs

Most past tense verbs are formed by adding **-ed** to the present tense forms.
Irregular verbs are not.

Example of an irregular verb:

	Present Tense	Past Tense	Past with Has or Have
	I <u>go</u> today.	I <u>went</u> yesterday.	I <u>have gone</u> before.

Pelé

Fill in the chart with the correct forms of each
irregular verb. Refer to a dictionary if needed.

Present	Past	Past with Has or Have
1. forgive	_____	_____
2. lose	_____	_____
3. tell	_____	_____
4. ring	_____	_____
5. sew	_____	_____
6. give	_____	_____

Write the past tense of each irregular verb in parentheses.

7. Phil _____ about Pelé, the greatest soccer player of all times. (read)

8. Pelé _____ up in Brazil. (grow)

9. He _____ playing professional soccer in 1956. (begin)

10. Pelé _____ every scoring record in Brazil. (hold)

11. His team _____ five South American Championships. (win)

12. Pelé _____ his team to three World Cup Championships. (lead)

13. He _____ an international hero. (is)

14. The President of France _____ Pelé a Knight of the Order of Merit. (make)

15. Pelé _____ his Brazilian team after 18 years. (leave)

16. He _____ to the U.S.A. in 1975 and played for New York. (come)

Name

Irregular verbs

Most past tense verbs are formed by adding **-ed** to the present tense forms.
Irregular verbs are not.

Example of an irregular verb:	**Present Tense**	**Past Tense**	**Past With Has or Have**
	I <u>go</u> today.	I <u>went</u> yesterday.	I <u>have gone</u> before.

Leonardo, the Inventor

Write the past tense of each irregular verb in parentheses. Refer to a dictionary
if needed.

1. Leonardo da Vinci _____ notes about his discoveries. (keep)

2. He _____ his notes in mirror writing. (make)

3. Leonardo da Vinci _____ about the power of water and what it
   could do. (think)

4. He _____ much about the human body. (know)

5. Leonardo _____ sketches of bones, muscles, and organs. (draw)

6. He watched birds and _____ how they could glide and land. (see)

7. Leonardo da Vinci _____ people would someday be able to fly like
   birds. (feel)

8. He invented an "airscrew" that _____ the basis of the helicopter.
   (become)

9. Leonardo never _____ many of this inventions. (build)

10. However, his ideas _____ to the development of machines used
    today. (lead)

On another sheet of paper, write a
sentence for each of the three forms
of the irregular verbs below.

Example: I **sing** well. I **sang** in the
school music program. I **have
sung** in public many times.

1. wear, worn, (has, have) worn

2. fly, flew, (has, have) flown

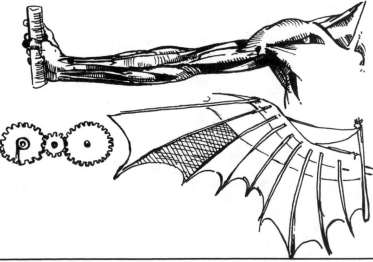

Name _____

Subject/verb agreement

The **verb** in the predicate of a sentence **must agree** with the **subject** of the sentence.

If the subject is singular, add **-s** or **-es** to most present tense verbs.
Example: Pollution kills animals and plants in the oceans.

If the subject is plural, the main present tense verb does not change.
Example: People cause pollution of the oceans.

Pollution Problems

Write the verb in parentheses that agrees with the
subject of each sentence.

1. Oceans _____ more than seven-
   tenths of Earth's surface. (cover, covers)

2. The seas _____ over 90 percent
   of Earth's water. (contain, contains)

3. More than half the people on Earth _____
   on or near the sea coasts. (live, lives)

4. Oceans _____ Earth's climate. (affect, affects)

5. An enormous amount of food _____ from the oceans. (come, comes)

6. Pollution _____ the animals that live in the sea. (damage, damages)

7. Chemicals and pesticides used in farming _____ the rivers.
   (pollute, pollutes)

8. Rivers _____ topsoil and waste to the oceans. (carry, carries)

9. Oil spills _____ wildlife and ruin beaches. (kill, kills)

10. People _____ trash and litter into our oceans. (dump, dumps)

11. Trash _____ problems for sea animals. (create, creates)

12. Birds and fish can _____ if they get caught in plastic packaging.
    (drown, drowns)

13. Plastic _____ very slowly, and it may be in the ocean over 100 years.
    (decay, decays)

14. The government _____ the dumping of garbage in the oceans.
    (prohibit, prohibits)

Name

Subject/verb agreement

The **verb** in the predicate of a sentence **must agree** with the **subject** of the sentence.

If the subject is singular, add **-s** to most present tense verbs.
Example: A saguaro <u>cactus</u> <u>grows</u> slowly.

If the subject is plural, the main present tense verb does not change.
Example: Saguaro <u>cactuses</u> <u>grow</u> slowly.

A compound subject has two or more simple subjects joined by *and*. It is like a plural subject. The main present tense verb does not change. Example: The <u>saguaro</u> *and* other <u>cactuses</u> <u>produce</u> flowers.

Verbs must agree with subject pronouns. Add **-s** or **-es** to most present tense verbs when the subject pronoun is *she, he,* or *it*. The main verb does not change when the subject pronoun is *I, we, you,* or *they*. Example: <u>They</u> <u>produce</u> flowers.

A Prickly Subject

Write the verb that agrees with the subject of each sentence.

1. Most cactuses _____ in hot, dry regions. (grow, grows)

2. They _____ in size and shape. (vary, varies)

3. The height of a giant saguaro _____ 60 feet. (reach, reaches)

4. Some varieties of cactuses _____ like tiny pincushions. (look, looks)

5. Thick, fleshy stems and long roots _____ cactuses survive. (help, helps)

6. The stem _____ water. (hold, holds)

7. The cactus's waxy skin _____ water from evaporating. (keep, keeps)

8. Its long roots _____ water after a rain. (absorb, absorbs)

9. A cactus's spines _____ it from being eaten by animals. (protect, protects)

10. They _____ in clusters out of little bumps on the stem. (grow, grows)

11. The bumps _____ in regular patterns on most cactuses. (occur, occurs)

Sentence combining: nouns in a series

Unit 7

Combine sentences with related ideas to make one better sentence. You can **combine three or more nouns** in the **subject** of a sentence. Use commas to separate the nouns. Use *and* before the last noun. Example: <u>Apples</u> are fruits. <u>Pears</u> are fruits. <u>Peaches</u> are fruits. (These sentences have related ideas. Avoid unnecessary repetition by combining the nouns.) <u>Apples</u>, <u>pears</u>, *and* <u>peaches</u> are fruits.

You can **combine three or more nouns** in the **predicate** of a sentence. Example: Maria picks <u>apples</u>. Maria picks <u>pears</u>. Maria picks <u>peaches</u>. (These sentences have related ideas. Avoid unnecessary repetition by combining the nouns.) Maria picks <u>apples</u>, <u>pears</u>, *and* <u>peaches</u>.

Down on the Farm

Read each set of sentences. Combine the nouns in the subjects or the nouns in the predicates to write a better sentence.

1. Jim liked to visit Grandma and Grandpa. Sean liked to visit Grandma and Grandpa. Maria liked to visit Grandma and Grandpa.

   _____

2. Grandpa had horses on his farm. Grandpa had cows. Grandpa had pigs.

   _____

3. Grandma raised chickens. Grandma raised ducks. Grandma raised geese.

   _____

4. Daisies grew in her garden. Tulips grew her garden. Roses grew in her garden.

   _____

5. Jim and Sean planted tomatoes. Jim and Sean planted green peppers. Jim and Sean planted carrots in the garden.

   _____

6. Maria grew beautiful daffodils. Maria grew beautiful snapdragons. Maria grew beautiful marigolds.

   _____

On another sheet of paper, write a sentence with a series of three nouns in the subject. Then write a sentence with a series of three nouns in the predicate. Remember to use commas correctly.

103

Sentence combining: verbs in a series

Unit 7

Combine sentences with related ideas to make one better sentence. You can **combine three or more verbs** in the **predicate** of a sentence. Use commas to separate the verbs. Use *and* before the last verb. Example: Rob <u>chose a topic</u>. Rob <u>read a book</u>. Rob <u>took notes for a report</u>. (These sentences have related ideas. Avoid unnecessary repetition by combining the verbs.) Rob <u>chose a topic</u>, <u>read a book</u>, **and** <u>took notes for a report</u>.

Rob's Report

Read each set of sentences. Combine the verbs in the predicates to write a better sentence.

1. Rob studied his notes. He organized them. He wrote an outline.

   _____

2. Rob wrote a rough draft. Rob revised it. Rob proofread it.

   _____

3. Rob made corrections. He copied the report. He shared it with the class.

   _____

4. Rob reported about Yosemite National Park. He showed pictures of the park. He gave its history.

   _____

5. The students listened carefully. The students asked questions. The students learned about Yosemite National Park.

   _____

6. Rob smiled. He thanked the class for their attention. He returned to his seat.

   _____

On another sheet of paper, write three sentences, each with a different action verb, about a related idea. Then combine them into one sentence.

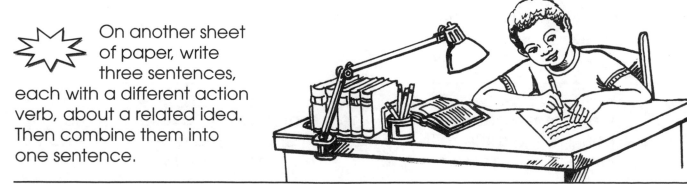

Sentence combining with adjectives and adverbs   Unit 7

More than one **adjective** can describe the same noun.
Example: Crater Lake is a <u>beautiful</u> *lake*. Crater Lake is a <u>blue</u> *lake*.

The subject of the two sentences is the same. The adjectives describe the same noun in the predicate. Combine the two sentences to make a better sentence. Use a comma or *and* between the adjectives. Example: Crater Lake is a <u>beautiful</u>, <u>blue</u> *lake*. Crater Lake is a <u>beautiful</u> *and* <u>blue</u> *lake*.

More than one **adverb** can describe the action of the same verb. Example: Rita and I *walked* <u>slowly</u> down the trail. Rita and I *walked* <u>carefully</u> down the trail.

The subject of the two sentences is the same. The adverbs describe the action of the same verb in the predicate. Combine the sentences to make a better sentence. Use *and* between the adverbs. Example: Rita and I *walked* <u>slowly</u> *and* <u>carefully</u> down the trail.

Crater Lake

Read each pair of sentences.
Combine the adjectives or adverbs
with **and** to write a better sentence.

1. The trail was narrow. The trail was rocky.

   _____

2. The trail zig-zagged steeply. The trail zig-zagged sharply to the left.

   _____

3. Rita nervously watched the edge. Rita intently watched the edge of the trail.

   _____

4. The trail suddenly ended at the dock. The trail abruptly ended at the dock.

   _____

5. We saw a breathtaking sight. We saw a spectacular sight.

   _____

6. Crater Lake is a sapphire-blue color. Crater Lake is extremely clear.

   _____

On another sheet of paper, write a sentence with two adjectives that describe the same noun. Underline the two adjectives. Then write a sentence with two adverbs that describe the action of the same verb. Circle each adverb.

Name

Expanding sentences with adjectives and adverbs

An **adjective** is a word that describes a noun. It tells how many or what kind. Using adjectives in your writing can make it more interesting and colorful. An adjective is often used in front of the noun it describes.
Example: A pineapple is a plant. A pineapple is a <u>tropical</u> plant.

An **adverb** is a word that describes the action of a verb. It tells how, when, or where the action of the verb takes place. An adverb may come before or after a verb.
Example: Mother bought a pineapple. Mother bought a pineapple <u>today</u>.

Pineapple Plant

Write the correct adjective or adverb in parentheses to complete each sentence.

1. A pineapple has a _____ fruit. (juicy, just)

2. The plant grows about _____ feet tall. (totally, two)

3. The top of a pineapple has a group of _____ leaves. (small, soon)

4. The flesh of the pineapple is _____ yellow. (plainly, pale)

5. Most of the plant's roots grow _____. (underground, usual)

6. Pineapple plants need a _____ climate. (warmly, warm)

7. The soil must be _____. (well, well-drained)

8. The farmers plow the land _____. (deeply, deep)

9. They break up the soil _____. (well, wonderful)

10. Pineapples can be grown from any

    of _____ parts of the plant. (four, for)

11. The new plants must be tended

    _____. (careful, carefully)

12. Weeding, spraying, and fertilizing is done

    by machines _____. (now, new)

13. It takes about _____ months for a

    pineapple to mature. (twenty, there)

Name

Using exact nouns and verbs

A **noun** is a word that names a person, place, or thing. In speaking and writing,
try to be as exact as possible to make your ideas clear and precise.

Example: The boy went to the store. (The sentence does not give exact information.)
Carlos went to the supermarket. (These nouns tell exactly who went where.)

A **verb** is a word that describes the action of the noun. Use exact verbs to make your ideas clear.

Example: Carlos went to the supermarket. (The verb is not as exact as it could be.)
Carlos ran to the supermarket. (*Ran* tells exactly how Carlos went to the supermarket.)

A Busy Day for Carlos

Write the exact noun in parentheses to complete each sentence.

1. Carlos selected some _____. (fruit, apples)

2. He chose two _____. (carrots, vegetables)

3. He picked up a carton of _____. (milk, liquid)

4. Carlos put some _____ into his shopping cart. (dessert, cookies)

5. Carlos paid the _____ for the items. (person, cashier)

6. He carried the _____ home. (groceries, things)

Choose an exact verb from the Word Bank to replace **went** in ARKET
each sentence. Write the new sentence on another sheet of paper.

scampered	played	dived
chased	rode	jogged

7. Later Carlos **went** to the park on his bike.

8. Some children **went** in the sandbox.

9. A collie **went** after a ball.

10. Mr. Randall **went** down the hill.

11. A squirrel **went** up a tree.

12. Carlos **went** in the swimming pool.

Name _____

Using exact adjectives and adverbs   Unit 7

An **adjective** is a word that describes a noun. Some adjectives like *nice* and *pretty* are overused. Try to be as exact as possible in writing and speaking to make your ideas clear and precise. Example: My family and I went to a <u>nice</u> concert. My family and I went to a <u>spectacular</u> concert.

An **adverb** describes the action of the verb. Some adverbs like *well* and *nicely* are overused. Try to be as exact as possible in writing and speaking to make your ideas clear and precise. Example: The orchestra played <u>well</u>. The orchestra played <u>beautifully</u>.

Majestic Music

Write the correct exact adjective or exact adverb in parentheses to complete each sentence.

1. The concert hall was _____. (pretty, fabulous)

2. It was _____ decorated in red velvet and gold. (ornately, nicely)

3. The audience waited _____ for the concert to begin. (eagerly, happily)

4. The _____ conductor raised his baton. (young, thirty-year-old)

5. The _____ orchestra came to attention. (big, huge)

6. The audience was _____ still. (very, absolutely)

7. The orchestra performed _____. (magnificently, well)

8. The tenor sang _____. (nicely, brilliantly)

9. The audience clapped _____. (enthusiastically, loudly)

10. It was a _____ concert. (good, splendid)

Choose the exact adjective or adverb for each phrase. Underline your choice.

11. a harp's (soft, delicate) tones

12. a (difficult, hard) composition

13. sang (well, beautifully)

14. a (world-famous, well-known) orchestra

15. reacted (joyously, nicely)

Using good and bad correctly

Unit 7

Good is an adjective that describes a noun. Use **better** to compare two nouns. Use **best** to compare more than two nouns. **Bad** is an adjective that describes a noun. Use **worse** to compare two nouns. Use **worst** to compare more than two nouns. Examples: The forecaster reported <u>good</u> weather for our town. Unfortunately, some places will have <u>bad</u> weather.

Forms of *good* and *bad* are used after linking verbs to describe the noun. (However, do not use *good* and *bad* after a linking verb to describe someone's health.) Examples: Our weather is <u>good</u>. The weather is <u>better</u> today than yesterday.

Weather-Wise

Complete each sentence with the correct form of good or bad in parentheses.

1. The forecaster said our weather will be _____ on Thursday than today. (good, better, best)

2. She said the _____ weather will be over the weekend. (good, better, best)

3. I feel _____ about that. (good, better, best)

4. Parts of the country are having _____ storms. (bad, worse, worst)

5. Fargo has had a _____ winter than it had last year. (bad, worse, worst)

6. The forecaster is predicting the _____ snow is yet to come. (bad, worse, worst)

7. Florida usually has _____ winter weather. (good, better, best)

8. I think Florida has the _____ temperatures of all the states. (good, better, best)

9. When northern states are having _____ weather, Florida has sunshine. (bad, worse, worst)

10. Let's go to Florida where the weather is always _____ . (good, better, best)

Name _____

Using well and bad correctly

Well is an adverb that describes the action of a verb. Use **better** to compare two verbs. Use **best** to compare more than two verbs. **Badly** is an adverb that describes the action of a verb. Use **worse** to compare two verbs. Use **worst** to compare more than two actions. Examples: The Saturns played <u>badly</u>. The Martians played much <u>better</u> than the Saturns.

Well is an adjective when it is used to describe someone's health. *Better* and *best* are the comparative forms. Example: The Martians' pitcher is <u>well</u> after having elbow surgery.

Martians vs. Saturns

Complete each sentence with the correct form of well or badly in parentheses.

1. The baseball game went _____ for the Martians right from the first inning. (well, better, best)

2. The first batter, Monroe, always hits _____. (well, better, best)

3. The Saturns' pitcher pitched _____ to Monroe, and he hit a double. (badly, worse, worst)

4. Monroe runs the bases _____ than most players on his team. (well, better, best)

5. Stanley, the second batter, usually hits even _____ than Monroe. (well, better, best)

6. The pitcher threw _____ pitches to Stanley than he did to Monroe. (badly, worse, worst)

7. Stanley hit the ball _____, and it flew over the fence for a two-run homer. (well, better, best)

8. Things went _____ for the Saturns in the second inning than in the first. (badly, worse, worst)

9. Now, their coach knew _____ what had to be done. (well, better, best)

10. He replaced the pitcher, and things went _____ for the Saturns. (well, better, best)

Name

Using negatives correctly

A **negative** is a word used to make a sentence mean **"no."** *No, no one, not, nothing, never, nobody, nowhere,* and contractions formed from a verb and *not* are negative words.

Only use one negative word in a sentence. Example: I have <u>never</u> seen live flamingos.

A **double negative** is the incorrect use of two negative words in a sentence.
Example: I have <u>never</u> seen <u>no</u> live flamingos.

The sentence can be corrected by either removing *no* or by replacing *no* with *any.*
Example: I have <u>never</u> seen <u>any</u> live flamingos.

Fantastic Flamingos

Study the chart showing words that can replace a second negative in a sentence. Then replace the second negative in each sentence below with a word from the chart.

Negative	Positive	Negative	Positive
no, none	a, any, one	nobody	anybody, somebody
no one	anyone, someone	nowhere	anywhere, somewhere
nothing	anything, something	never	ever

1. There aren't flamingos living nowhere by me.

_____

2. Can't nobody tell me where they live?

_____

3. There aren't no other wading birds as big and colorful.

_____

4. I don't know of no birds besides flamingos that eat upside-down.

_____

5. I wouldn't never think it possible for a bird to eat so much algae.

_____

6. I never saw none other birds stand on one leg like flamingos.

_____

7. There must not be nothing else like flamingos.

_____

Name

Read or listen to the directions. Fill in the circle beside the best answer.

☐ Example:

Which is not true of homophones?

(A) They are words that sound the same.

(B) They are words that are spelled the same.

(C) They are words that have different meanings.

Take time to review your answers.

Answer: B because homophones are spelled differently.

Now try these. You have 20 minutes. Continue until you see ⬡STOP .

Which set of words is not a pair of homophones?

1.
(A) band, banned
(B) paced, paste
(C) weigh, weight
(D) tears, tiers

2.
(A) cause, caws
(B) both, bath
(C) not, knot
(D) toe, tow

---

3. Which sentence does not contain a pair of homophones?

(A) We'd better weed the garden today.

(B) I'll walk down the aisle slowly.

(C) I wrote Mandi a note.

(D) Have you seen the scene I drew?

4. In which sentence is the pronoun **me** used correctly?

(A) Fred and me picked blueberries Saturday.

(B) Mom was glad me and Fred picked them.

(C) Mom made a blueberry pie for Fred and me.

(D) Me and Fred ate the whole pie.

5. Which pronoun could correctly replace the underlined words in the sentence?

Keith got <u>all the multiplication problems</u> correct.

It
(A)

they
(B)

his
(C)

NG
(D)

6. In which sentence is a form of the irregular verb **fly** used correctly?

(A) The honeybee fly yesterday.

(B) She flew from flower to flower collecting pollen.

(C) Then she flewed back to the beehive.

(D) Other honeybees then flown to other flowers.

7. Which sentence has an irregular verb?

(A) Dad called loudly for the boys.   (B) He shouted again.

(C) At last the boys heard him.   (D) They all walked home.

8. In which sentence does the verb not agree with the subject?

(A) Spiders' jaws moves from side to side.   (B) Spiders eat insects.

(C) Spiders' bodies have two sections.   (D) Spiders drink their food.

GO ON

9. In which sentence does the verb agree with the subject?

    Ⓐ Fruit-eating bats sees very well.

    Ⓑ Bats catches flying insects at night.

    Ⓒ Many bats live in caves.

    Ⓓ Bats hunts for food at night.

10. Which is the correct way to combine the three sentences below?

    The stonefish is a poisonous fish. The scorpionfish is a poisonous fish. The pufferfish is a poisonous fish.

    Ⓐ The stonefish, the scorpionfish, and the pufferfish are poisonous fish.

    Ⓑ The stonefish is a poisonous fish and the scorpionfish and the pufferfish.

    Ⓒ The stonefish and the scorpionfish and the pufferfish are poisonous fish.

    Ⓓ The stonefish and the scorpionfish are poisonous fish and the pufferfish.

11. Which is the correct way to combine the three sentences below?

    My family has a picnic on Independence Day. My family goes swimming on Independence Day. We watch fireworks on Independence Day.

    Ⓐ My family has a picnic and goes swimming and watches fireworks on Independence Day.

    Ⓑ My family has a picnic, goes swimming, and watches fireworks on Independence Day.

    Ⓒ My family has a picnic goes, swimming and watches fireworks on Independence Day.

    Ⓓ My family has a picnic goes swimming, and watches fireworks on Independence Day.

GO ON

114

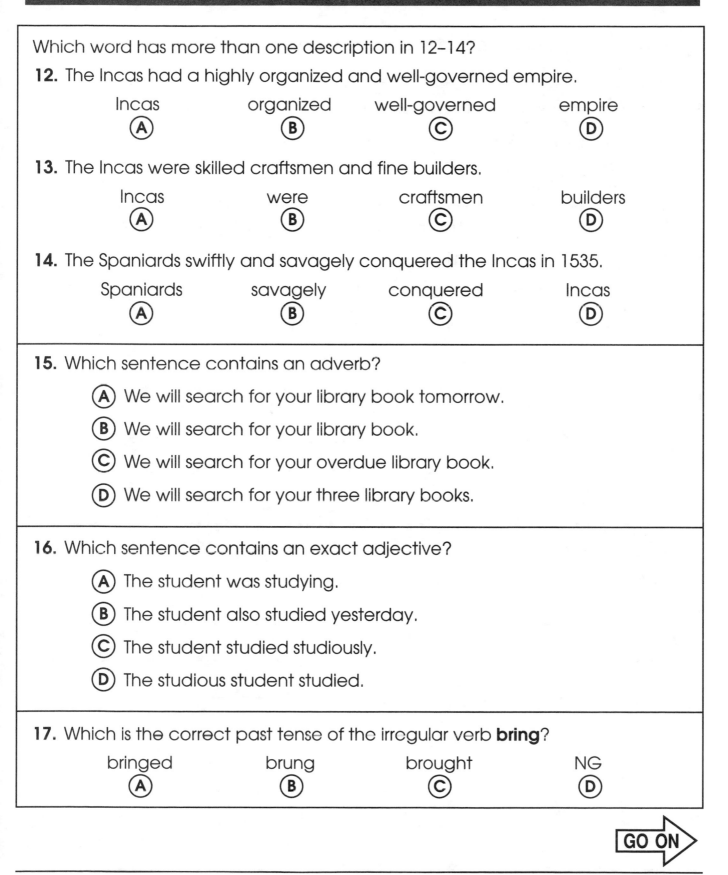

Which word has more than one description in 12–14?

12. The Incas had a highly organized and well-governed empire.

Incas	organized	well-governed	empire
Ⓐ	Ⓑ	Ⓒ	Ⓓ

13. The Incas were skilled craftsmen and fine builders.

Incas	were	craftsmen	builders
Ⓐ	Ⓑ	Ⓒ	Ⓓ

14. The Spaniards swiftly and savagely conquered the Incas in 1535.

Spaniards	savagely	conquered	Incas
Ⓐ	Ⓑ	Ⓒ	Ⓓ

15. Which sentence contains an adverb?

Ⓐ We will search for your library book tomorrow.

Ⓑ We will search for your library book.

Ⓒ We will search for your overdue library book.

Ⓓ We will search for your three library books.

16. Which sentence contains an exact adjective?

Ⓐ The student was studying.

Ⓑ The student also studied yesterday.

Ⓒ The student studied studiously.

Ⓓ The studious student studied.

17. Which is the correct past tense of the irregular verb **bring**?

bringed	brung	brought	NG
Ⓐ	Ⓑ	Ⓒ	Ⓓ

GO ON

18. Which sentence contains two exact nouns?

Ⓐ The officer rode a vehicle.

Ⓑ The person rode a motorcycle.

Ⓒ The officer rode a motorcycle.

Ⓓ He rode it.

19. Which sentence contains an exact adjective and an exact adverb?

Ⓐ The beautiful ballerina danced gracefully.

Ⓑ The pretty ballerina danced gracefully.

Ⓒ The beautiful ballerina danced nicely.

Ⓓ The pretty ballerina danced nicely.

20. Which form of **good** would complete the sentence correctly?

These are the _____ chocolate chip cookies you have ever baked.

good	better	best	bestest
Ⓐ	Ⓑ	Ⓒ	Ⓓ

Explain what is incorrect in the sentence below and how it can be corrected.

George hasn't never sung better than he did today.

_____

_____

_____

STOP

Final Review Test Name Grid

Write your name in pencil in the boxes along the top. Begin with your last name. Fill in as many letters as will fit. Then follow the columns straight down and bubble in the letters that correspond with the letters in your name. Complete the rest of the information the same way. You may use a piece of scrap paper to help you keep your place.

STUDENT'S NAME			SCHOOL
LAST	FIRST	MI	TEACHER

FEMALE ○   MALE ○

DATE OF BIRTH

MONTH	DAY	YEAR

(Name grid bubbles A–Z for each letter column)

MONTH	DAY		YEAR	
JAN ○	⓪	⓪	⓪	⓪
FEB ○	①	①	①	①
MAR ○	②	②	②	②
APR ○	③	③	③	③
MAY ○		④	④	④
JUN ○		⑤	⑤	⑤
JUL ○		⑥	⑥	⑥
AUG ○		⑦	⑦	⑦
SEP ○		⑧	⑧	⑧
OCT ○		⑨	⑨	⑨
NOV ○				
DEC ○				

GRADE ③ ④ ⑤

Final Review Test Answer Sheet

Pay close attention when transferring your answers. Fill in the bubbles neatly and completely. You may use a piece of scrap paper to help you keep your place.

SAMPLES
A Ⓐ Ⓑ ● Ⓓ
B Ⓕ ● Ⓗ Ⓙ

1 Ⓐ Ⓑ Ⓒ Ⓓ
2 Ⓕ Ⓖ Ⓗ Ⓙ
3 Ⓐ Ⓑ Ⓒ Ⓓ
4 Ⓕ Ⓖ Ⓗ Ⓙ
5 Ⓐ Ⓑ Ⓒ Ⓓ
6 Ⓕ Ⓖ Ⓗ Ⓙ

7 Ⓐ Ⓑ Ⓒ Ⓓ
8 Ⓕ Ⓖ Ⓗ Ⓙ
9 Ⓐ Ⓑ Ⓒ Ⓓ
10 Ⓕ Ⓖ Ⓗ Ⓙ
11 Ⓐ Ⓑ Ⓒ Ⓓ
12 Ⓕ Ⓖ Ⓗ Ⓙ

13 Ⓐ Ⓑ Ⓒ Ⓓ
14 Ⓕ Ⓖ Ⓗ Ⓙ
15 Ⓐ Ⓑ Ⓒ Ⓓ
16 Ⓕ Ⓖ Ⓗ Ⓙ
17 Ⓐ Ⓑ Ⓒ Ⓓ
18 Ⓕ Ⓖ Ⓗ Ⓙ

19 Ⓐ Ⓑ Ⓒ Ⓓ
20 Ⓕ Ⓖ Ⓗ Ⓙ
21 Ⓐ Ⓑ Ⓒ Ⓓ
22 Ⓕ Ⓖ Ⓗ Ⓙ
23 Ⓐ Ⓑ Ⓒ Ⓓ
24 Ⓕ Ⓖ Ⓗ Ⓙ

25 Ⓐ Ⓑ Ⓒ Ⓓ
26 Ⓕ Ⓖ Ⓗ Ⓙ
27 Ⓐ Ⓑ Ⓒ Ⓓ
28 Ⓕ Ⓖ Ⓗ Ⓙ
29 Ⓐ Ⓑ Ⓒ Ⓓ
30 Ⓕ Ⓖ Ⓗ Ⓙ

Name

Read or listen to the directions. Fill in the circle beside the best answer.

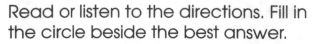 Example:

Which word is not a common noun?

(A) castle   (B) drawbridge

(C) Arthur   (D) knights

Answer: C because it names a special person and begins with a capital letter.

Now try these. You have 30 minutes.

Continue until you see ⬡STOP .

Remember your Helping Hand Strategies:

1. Cross out answers you know are wrong.

2. Use your time wisely. If a question seems too tough, skip it and come back to it later.

3. Take time to review your answers.

4. Transfer your answers carefully. Use a piece of scratch paper to keep you

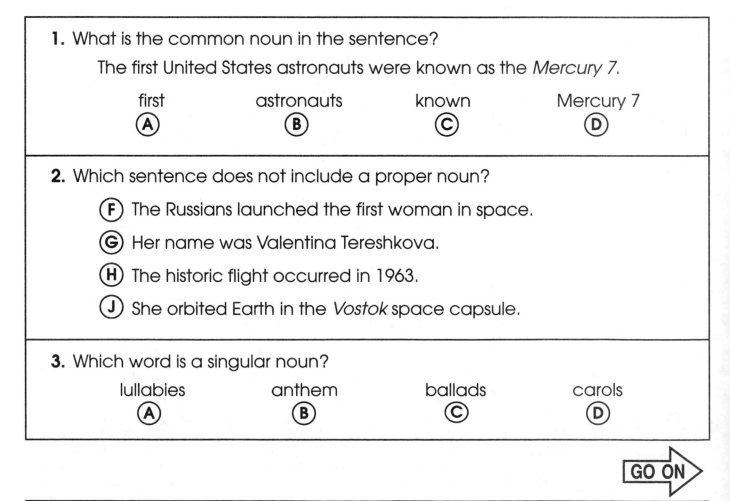

1. What is the common noun in the sentence?

The first United States astronauts were known as the *Mercury 7*.

first	astronauts	known	Mercury 7
(A)	(B)	(C)	(D)

2. Which sentence does not include a proper noun?

(F) The Russians launched the first woman in space.

(G) Her name was Valentina Tereshkova.

(H) The historic flight occurred in 1963.

(J) She orbited Earth in the *Vostok* space capsule.

3. Which word is a singular noun?

lullabies	anthem	ballads	carols
(A)	(B)	(C)	(D)

GO ON ➤

4. Which word Is not a plural noun?

men
(F)

people
(G)

widows
(H)

person
(J)

5. Which word is the correct possessive form of **women**?

woman's
(A)

womens'
(B)

women's
(C)

NG
(D)

6. Choose the correct pronoun for the underlined words.

My uncle likes to take <u>Dennis and me</u> bowling.

us
(F)

you
(G)

him
(H)

them
(J)

7. Which sentence does not have an action verb?

(A) The ambulance rushed the man to the hospital.

(B) He was unconscious.

(C) The emergency room doctor saved the man's life.

(D) He recovered from his injuries.

8. Which is the correct past tense of **build**?

build
(F)

builded
(G)

builder
(H)

NG
(J)

9. Which sentence has a helping verb and an action verb?

(A) Mr. Groves was late for the hockey game.

(B) He was driving too fast.

(C) He got a speeding ticket.

(D) Mr. Groves arrived late to the game.

GO ON

Final Review Test

10. Which sentence has a future tense verb?

(F) Fiona and I have saved our money.

(G) We want to see the new movie.

(H) We will go tomorrow.

(J) I hope the movie is still playing.

11. Which sentence does not have a contraction?

(A) Leonardo da Vinci's Mona Lisa is a remarkable painting.

(B) It's kept in a museum in Paris.

(C) We'd have to go to France to see it.

(D) I guess I'll have to wait to see it.

12. Which word is not an adjective?

Barney plays a shiny brass tuba in the big parade.

shiny	brass	tuba	big
(F)	(G)	(H)	(J)

13. Which adverb will correctly complete the sentence?

Mr. Adams drove the car _____ on the icy road.

(A) cautiously   (B) more cautiously

(C) most cautiously   (D) NG

14. Identify the sentence below.

Help me unload the truck.

(F) declarative   (G) interrogative

(H) exclamatory   (J) NG

GO ON

Final Review Test

15. Which sentence has the complete subject underlined?

(A) <u>Two French inventors proved that hot-air</u> balloons could fly.

(B) <u>They</u> sent animals up in a balloon in 1783.

(C) <u>Then two men volunteered</u> to be the first humans to go up in a balloon.

(D) <u>They successfully floated above Paris</u> for 25 minutes.

16. Which sentence has the complete predicate underlined?

(F) <u>The pyramids of Egypt</u> have fascinated people for centuries.

(G) The most famous <u>are those standing at Giza</u>.

(H) <u>They were built</u> for the pharaohs 4,500 years ago.

(J) The pharaohs were <u>looked upon as gods</u>.

17. Which sentence is a compound sentence?

(A) Catherine the Great ruled Russia for 34 years.

(B) She became tsarina after her husband, Tsar Peter, was killed.

(C) Catherine encouraged learning, and she adopted Western European culture.

(D) She collected great works of art that can be seen in museums today.

18. Which sentence is not written correctly?

(F) A spider's body is covered with tough skin.

(G) Is the shell called an exoskeleton!

(H) Does a spider have a nose or a tongue?

(J) Wow, most spiders have eight eyes!

Final Review Test

19. Which quotation is written correctly?

(A) "Sailfish can swim very fast said Mr. Carr."

(B) Dan asked "How fast can they swim?"

(C) Mr. Carr answered, "They can go almost 70 miles per hour."

(D) Sailfish can only go that fast for short distances, he said.

20. Which sentence is not written correctly?

(F) Alneta's birthday is Wednesday, March 17.

(G) That is the same day as St. Patrick's day.

(H) Alneta lives at 7708 Oxford Avenue.

(J) Is that in Portland, Oregon, or Portland, Maine?

21. Which sentence is written correctly?

(A) Sandie has read the book The Starplace two times.

(B) She likes the magazine Zillions.

(C) Sandie's favorite song is "Castle on a Cloud."

(D) The Jumblies, a poem by Edward Lear, is her favorite poem.

22. In which sentence is each comma used correctly?

(F) Capybaras are mammals, like whales, dogs, and humans.

(G) Capybaras, gerbils, squirrels, and mice are rodents.

(H) They are the largest, rodents, and weigh up to 140 pounds.

(J) Capybaras live in the grasslands, of Venezuela in South America.

23. In which sentence is the apostrophe not used correctly?

(A) Mr. Marcus's new sports car is blue.

(B) I'd like to ride in it.

(C) He'll take you for a ride soon.

(D) Sports cars' can go very fast.

24. Which sentence does not contain a pair of homophones?

(F) It is plain to see the plane did not arrive on time.

(G) Who knows how the boy hurt his nose?

(H) Paul acts like the ax is too heavy.

(J) Jennie has some of the same books I have.

25. In which sentence does the verb not agree with the subject?

(A) Honeybees lives in colonies.

(B) Colonies are large groups of bees.

(C) There may be 50,000 bees living together in a colony.

(D) Each bee has a special job to do.

26. Which part of speech is underlined?

The study of <u>artificial</u> intelligence is fascinating.

noun (F)   verb (G)   adjective (H)   adverb (J)

27. Which part of speech is underlined?

Some scientists think machines will think <u>better</u> than humans someday.

noun (A)   verb (B)   adjective (C)   adverb (D)

GO ON →

Final Review Test

28. Which sentence contains an exact adjective and an exact adverb?

(F) Marla proudly accepted the big trophy.

(G) Marla accepted the big trophy.

(H) Marla accepted the huge trophy.

(J) Marla proudly accepted the huge trophy.

29. Which sentence uses the correct form of **bad**?

(A) This is the worse book I have ever read.

(B) It is even worst than the author's last book.

(C) For one thing, the plot is bad.

(D) I do not want to read any more worse books.

30. Which sentence has a double negative?

(F) I don't see any sunshine.

(G) I hope it doesn't rain.

(H) A picnic is never much fun in the rain.

(J) Didn't nobody listen to the forecast?

Write a sentence that uses at least two capitalization rules and two punctuation rules. Then list the rules that were used.

_____

_____

_____

_____

Answer Key

Page 5

Persons: athlete, acrobat, diver, manager, senator, owner, directors; Places: valley, courtyard, hilltop, canyon, jungle, pasture, mountain; Things: buffalo, fountain, raccoon, wedding, feast, moment; 1.–4. Answers will vary.

Page 6

1. United States, Pennsylvania Avenue; 2. George Washington, President's House; 3. John Adams, Abigail; 4. President's House, War of 1812, President Monroe, 20th Street; 5. Andrew Jackson, President's Park; 6. President Roosevelt, White House; 7. White House, Executive Mansion; 8. Theodore Roosevelt, The White House Gang; 9. President Johnson, Rose Garden; 10. President George Bush, Gulf War; 11. President Clinton, Buddy; 12. Barbara, Jenna, President George W. Bush

Page 7

1. S; 2. P; 3. S; 4. P; 5. S; 6. S; 7. P; 8. P; 9. P; 10. S; 11. S; 12. P; 13. S; 14. S; 15. P; 16. P; 17. S; 18. S; 19. S; 20. P; 21. P; 22. S; 23. S; 24. P; 25. P; 26. P; 27. S; 28. P; 29. S; 30. P; 31. P; 32. S; 33. P; 34. P; 35. P; 36. P

Page 8

1. wagons; 2. glasses; 3. nieces; 4. trenches; 5. branches; 6. myths; 7. dresses; 8. marshes; 9. glaciers; 10. zippers; 11. speeches; 12. invitations; 13. wishes; 14. sleighs; 15. masks; 16. taxes; 17. buzzes; 18. brushes; 19. wrinkles; 20. patches; 21. mammals; 22. deserts; 23. forests; 24. pouches; 25. legs

Page 9

1. bunnies; 2. daisies; 3. ladies; 4. navies; 5. cities; 6. turkeys; 7. hobbies; 8. casualties; 9. puppies; 10. mummies; 11. copies; 12. libraries; 13. men; 14. children; 15. deer; 16. geese; 17. foot; 18. mice; 19. oxen; 20. women; 21. The men chased the oxen down the road.; 22. The women and the children fed the geese.

Page 10

1. tooth's; 2. Pacific's; 3. Yankees'; 4. players'; 5. men's; 6. reptiles'; 7. berries'; 8. course's; 9. plant's; 10. flowers'; 11. women's; 12. Paula's;

13. the ballerinas' dances; 14. the cookies' delicious taste; 15. the women's meeting; 16. the children's playground; 17. the Mets' win; 18. the rabbit's fluffy tail; 19. the pupils' pencils

Page 11

1. it; 2. it; 3. he; 4. we; 5. they; 6. she; 7. they; 8. he; 9. It; 10. They; 11. It; 12. She; 13. We; 14. He

Page 12

1. it; 2. it; 3. him; 4. them; 5. it; 6. them; 7. us; 8. her; 9. us; 10. them; 11. them; 12. him; 13. her; 14. it

Page 13

1. They; 2. It; 3. He; 4. it; 5. them; 6. them; 7. it

Page 14

1. Their; 2. Their; 3. its; 4. Its; 5. Her; 6. his; 7. Mine; 8. yours

Unit 1 Test

1. D; 2. D; 3. A; 4. C; 5. C; 6. B; 7. C; 8. C; 9. B; 10. A; 11. B; 12. C; 13. B; 14. C; 15. D; 16. B; 17. D; 18. B; 19. D; 20. B; Constructed-response answers will vary.

Page 19

1. no; 2. no; 3. yes; 4. yes; 5. yes; 6. yes; 7. yes; 8. yes; 9. yes; 10. no; 11. yes; 12. yes; 13. no; 14. yes; 15. yes; 16. no; 17. need; 18. use; 19. produce; 20. provide; 21. causes; 22. require; 23. face; 24. drill; 25. dam; 26. receive

Page 20

1. action; 2. neither; 3. action; 4. linking; 5. neither; 6. action; 7. action; 8. action; 9. linking; 10. linking; 11. is; 12. see; 13. lays; 14. hatch; 15. burrow; 16. eats; 17. builds; 18. grabs; 19. jumps; 20. appears

Page 21

1. explained; 2. hugged; 3. fanned; 4. twisted; 5. married; 6. studied; 7. destroyed; 8. denied; 9. hatched; 10. lived; 11. looked; 12. used; 13. breathed; 14. changed; 15. started; 16. flattened; 17. appeared; 18. vanished

Page 22

1. was, L; 2. became, L; 3. discovered, A; 4. created, A; 5. developed, A; 6. encouraged, A; 7. taught, A; 8. was,

L; 9. received, A; 10.–13. Answers will vary.

Page 23

1. wore; 2. sent; 3. grew; 4. caught; 5. forgave; 6. told; 7. spoke; 8. knew; 9. took; 10. lost; 11. stole; 12. won; 13. stuck; 14. swam; 15. sat; 16. stood; 17. gave

Page 24

1. HV = have, MV = provided; 2. HV = have, MV = lived; 3. HV = are, MV = making; 4. HV = is, MV = killing; 5. HV = are, MV = working; 6. HV = had, MV = made; 7. HV = is, MV = needed; 8. HV = will, MV = work; 9. past; 10. past; 11. present; 12. future; 13. future

Page 25

1. sang; 2. told; 3. bring; 4. worn; 5. took; 6. stand; 7. read; 8. known; 9. told; 10. said; 11. heard; 12. shown; 13. understood; 14. made

Page 26

1. would not; 2. have not; 3. are not; 4. does not; 5. hadn't; 6. didn't; 7. shouldn't; 8. hasn't; 9. she will; 10. he would; 11. you have; 12. she is; 13. you're; 14. she'd; 15. they've; 16. he'll

Unit 2 Test

1. B; 2. B; 3. C; 4. B; 5. A; 6. B; 7. C; 8. D; 9. C; 10. D; 11. A; 12. B; 13. B; 14. C; 15. B; 16. C; 17. A; 18. C; 19. C; 20. A; Constructed response: will play, It is in the future because of the words "next year."

Page 32

1. gentle, friendly; 2. big, beautiful; 3. soft, split, upper; 4. thick, wool; 5. soft; 6. easy; 7. long; 8. sure-footed; 9. wonderful, pack; 10. two-toed; 11. playful; 12. humming; 13. frightened

Page 33

1. Many; 2. Maple, sweet, delicious; 3. sugar, maple; 4. Pure, maple, expensive; 5. 40; 6. colorless, watery; 7. long, shallow; 8. pure, maple; 9. golden, brown; 10. artificial, maple

Page 34

1. more crumbly, most crumbly; 2. flatter, flattest; 3. braver, bravest; 4. more convenient, most convenient; 5. more graceful, most graceful; 6. more effective, most effective;

Answer Key

7. needier, neediest; 8. more dangerous; 9. dangerous; 10. most dangerous

Page 35

1. 1; 2. 2; 3. 3; 4. 2; 5. 2; 6. 2; 7. 3; 8. 1; 9. 2; 10. 1

Page 36

1. an; 2. a; 3. a; 4. a; 5. a; 6. the; 7. the; 8. the; 9. an; 10. a; 11. a; 12. an; 13. the; 14. a; 15. a; 16. an; 17. an; 18. a; 19. an; 20. a; 21. a; 22. an; 23. a; 24. a

Page 37

1. how; 2. how; 3. where; 4. when; 5. where; 6. where; 7. how; 8. how; 9. when; 10. where; 11. when; 12. –16. Answers will vary.

Page 38

1. down; 2. there; 3. carefully; 4. cautiously, away; 5. gently; 6. neatly; 7. Then; 8. once, freely; 9. everywhere; 10. greatly; 11. Next, nearby; 12. back, later

Page 39

1. more quietly, most quietly; 2. harder, hardest; 3. more frequently, most frequently; 4. longer, longest; 5. closer, closest; 6. more patiently, most patiently; 7. sooner, soonest; 8. patiently; 9. eagerly; 10. Soon; 11. more quickly; 12. broadly; 13. loudly

Unit 3 Test

1. B; 2. B; 3. A; 4. D; 5. C; 6. A; 7. B; 8. C; 9. C; 10. C; 11. B; 12. A; 13. B; 14. B; 15. D; 16. C; 17. B; 18. B; 19. A; 20. C; Constructed response: more rapidly; It compares two actions.

Page 44

1. D, .; 2. INT, ?; 3. D, .; 4. IMP, .; 5. D, .; 6. INT, ?; 7. E, !; 8. D, .; 9. IMP, .; 10. D, .; 11. INT, ?; 12. D, .; 13. E, !; 14. INT, ?; 15. D, .

Page 45

1. D; 2. D; 3. D; 4. I; 5. I; 6. D; 7. I; 8. D; 9. D; 10. I

Page 46

1. I, ?; 2. I, ?; 3. E, !; 4. E, !; 5. I, ?; 6. E, !; 7. I, ?; 8. I, ?; 9. I, ?; 10. E, !; 1.–3. Answers will vary.

Page 47

1. D; 2. F; 3. D; 4. F; 5. R; 6. D; 7. F; 8. D; 9. D; 10. F; 11. D; 12. R; Sentences will vary.

Page 48

1. SS = snowmobile, SP = is; 2. SS = persons, SP = ride; 3. SS = driver, SP = steers; 4. SS = Snowmobiles, SP = are; 5. SS = environmentalists, SP = believe; 6. SS = kind, SP = is; 7. SS = Toboggans, SP = are; 8. SS = wood, SP = allows; 9. SS = people, SP = ride; 10. SS = driver, SP = steers; 11. SS = Snowboarding, SP = became; 12. SS = Snowboards, SP = look; 13. SS = snowboarder, SP = does; 14. SS = Snowboarding, SP = became

Page 49

1. CS = A giant tortoise, SS = tortoise; 2. CS = Baby pandas, SS = pandas; 3. CS = These mammals, SS = mammals; 4. CS = An alligator's eye, SS = eye; 5. CS = Giraffes, SS = Giraffes; 6. CS = A sloth, SS = sloth; 7. CS = An elephant's trunk, SS = trunk; 8. CS = An octopus, SS = octopus; 9. CS = Octopuses, SS = Octopuses; 10. CS = A chameleon's tongue, SS = tongue; 11. CS = Dolphin brains, SS = brains; 12. CS = A hummingbird, SS = hummingbird; 13. CS = A horse's hoof, SS = hoof; 14. CS = A camel, SS = camel; 15. CS = The world's largest birds, SS = birds; 16. CS = Young gorillas, SS = gorillas

Page 50

1. CP = lives in a nest high in an old elm tree, SP = lives; 2. CP = awakens in his leafy nest early in the morning, SP = awakens; 3. CP = left earlier to look for food, SP = left; 4. CP = races along the elm's branches, SP = races; 5. CP = scampers down the tree trunk, SP = scampers; 6. CP = searches for some seeds he had buried, SP = searches; 7. CP = helps him find them, SP = helps; 8. CP = spies his brothers nearby, SP = spies; 9. CP = chatter back and forth, SP = chatter; 10. CP = chase one another all around, SP = chase; 11. CP = tires of the game, SP = tires; 12. CP = stretches out in the warm sun to rest, SP = stretches; 13.–16. Answers will vary.

Page 51

1. CP; 2. N; 3. CS; 4. CS; 5. N; 6. CS;

7. N; 8. CP; 9. N; 10. CP; 11. CP; 12. CS; 13. N; Answers will vary.

Page 52

1. Gordie Howe was known as "Mr. Hockey," and Wayne Gretzky was called "The Great One."; 2. Howe joined the Detroit Red Wings in 1946, and Gretzky began playing professionally in 1978.; 3. Howe spent most of his hockey career with the Red Wings, but Gretzky played with several different teams.; 4. Howe played right wing, and Gretzky was a center.; 5. Gordie Howe played hockey 26 seasons, but Wayne Gretzky only played for 20 seasons.

Page 53

1. Seven planets have moons that orbit them.; 2. Planets do not have their own light.; 3. Saturn has many rings around it.; 4. Is Saturn the second largest planet?; 5. Can you see Saturn's rings with a telescope?; 6. Was Saturn's biggest moon first seen in 1655?

Unit 4 Test

1. B; 2. B; 3. D; 4. A; 5. D; 6. D; 7. D; 8. B; 9. B; 10. B; 11. C; 12. C; 13. A; 14. B; 15. C; 16. A; 17. D; 18. C; 19. C; 20. B; Constructed-response answers will vary.

Midway Review Test

1. C; 2. G; 3. B; 4. H; 5. D; 6. G; 7. A; 8. G; 9. B; 10. H; 11. A; 12. G; 13. D; 14. H; 15. B; 16. J; 17. C; 18. F; 19. C; 20. J; Constructed response: compound sentence; Answers will vary.

Page 66

1. yes; 2. yes; 3. no; 4. yes; 5. no; 6. yes; 7. yes; 8. What; 9. They; 10. I; 11. There's; 12. "They wear comfortable clothes so they can exercise," explained Ms. Hill.; 13. Monroe asked, "Why do they have to exercise?"; 14. "Since there is so little gravity in space, the astronauts just float around."; 15. "Their muscles and bones would get weak if they did not exercise."

Page 67

1. no; 2. yes; 3. no; 4. yes; 5. yes; 6. yes; 7. no; 8. yes; 9. Cousin Sylvia; 10. Uncle Vernon; 11. Jerry Andrews; 12. Aunt Martha; 13. Paulo Jo Rollo; 14. Grandfather Murray; 15. B, C, D; 16. A, B, C, D; 17. none

Answer Key

Page 68

1. Mr. and Mrs. Foster; 2. Ms. Maxine Marshall; 3. Dr. C. L. Smith; 4. Miss Tiffany Tyler; 5. Mr. G. W. Abbott is my violin teacher.; 6. My soccer coach is Paul W. Young.; 7. Dr. Julia Fister is my dentist.

Page 69

1. Mrs. Wolf lived in Perryville, TN, and Oceanside, CA.; 2. Terri rode her bike from Ninth Street to Echo Hill Drive.; 3. Jupiter Island, Florida, is where my grandparents live.; 4. My aunt and uncle went to college in Iowa City, IA.; 5. Carter and his family drove to 927 Jenkins Lane in Pond, Mississippi.; 6. My Uncle Dwayne lives on Sunset Drive in Bartlesville, Oklahoma.; 7. Do you know if Connie lives on Sunshine Drive or Ridge Rd.?; 8. Mr. Hall's address is 1616 White Oaks Ave.; 9. Mary moved from Platte City, Missouri, to Lincoln, Nebraska.

Page 70

1. Basketball practices are on Thursdays and Saturdays.; 2. Seth is having friends spend the night on Wednesday for New Year's Eve.; 3. Laura's surprise party is Friday, February 5.; 4. My family celebrates Mother's Day and Thanksgiving Day at my aunt's house.; 5. This year Labor Day is Monday, September 3.; 6. Carole's birthday is next Saturday, March 12.; 7. Christmas Eve is always December 24.; 8. Presidents' Day is celebrated on the third Monday in February.

Page 71

1. PA = American; 2. PN = Minutemen, Lexington, Concord; PA = British; 3. PN = George Washington; PA = Continental; 4. PN = British, Battle of Bunker Hill; 5. PN = July, Congress, Declaration of Independence; 6. British troops occupied New York City in September, 1776.; 7. General Washington led the Americans to several victories in 1777.; 8. The British also won some battles, and they occupied Philadelphia.; 9. Then in 1778, France came to the aid of the United States.; 10. Cornwallis surrendered to the Americans at Yorktown in 1781.; 11. Great Britain and the United States signed a peace treaty on September 3, 1783.

Page 72

Friendly Letter: Primrose Lane, Bend, Oregon, August, Dear Barbara, I, There, I, I'll, I, Your, Bonnie; Business Letter: Ninth Street, Hillside, Maine, March, Mr. John Jones, Skateboards and More, Rock Ave., Detroit, Michigan, Dear Mr. Jones, I, It, Please, Sincerely, Sam Smith

Page 73

Abacus, History of the Abacus, A. Ancient, B. Used, The Abacus, A. Frame, B. Beads, C. Two, D. Numbers

Page 74

1. Sukey and the Mermaid; 2. Kids Discover; 3. Nowhere to Call Home; 4. Dave at Night; 5. Speed of Light; 6. Heart of a Tiger; 7. Tara read Julie of the Wolves by Jean Craighead.; 8. John said The View from Saturday is a good book.; 9. Did Karen Hess write Out of the Dust?; 10. Jamar enjoys reading U.S. Kids.; 11. Joe's favorite magazine is National Geographic World.

Page 75

1. "Loveliest of Trees"; 2. "Home on the Range"; 3. "If I Were a Bell"; 4. "The Fisherman and His Wife"; 5. "The Runaway"; 6. "Hummingbird Imposters"; 7. "This is My Country"; 8. "Primer Lesson"; 9. "Diving for Doubloons"; 10. "Mother to Son"

Unit 5 Test

1. C; 2. A; 3. B; 4. A; 5. D; 6. B; 7. C; 8. B; 9. A; 10. C; 11. A; 12. C; 13. D; 14. D; 15. A; 16. C; 17. C; 18. D; 19. C; 20. D; Constructed-response answers will vary.

Page 81

1. D; 2. C; 3. I; 4. D; 5. I; 6. D; 7. D; 8. C; 9. C; 10. D; 11.–14. Add a period to the end of each sentence.

Page 82

1. Mr. Carl L. Dyer; 2. Mr. and Mrs. W. W. Davis; 3. Rev. and Mrs. Pogue; 4. Ms. Janetta Lewis; 5. Dr. Greg T. Ward; 6. Miss Rita R. Reynolds; 7. Mon.; 8. Ln.; 9. Apr.; 10. Fri.; 11. Rd.; 12. Sat.; 13. Ct.; 14. Ave.; Feb.; Mrs. Cora K. Kramer, Tues., Mar.

Page 83

I., A., B., II., A., B., C., III., A., B., C.

Page 84

1. ?; 2. ?; 3. ?; 4. !; 5. !; 6. ?; 7. !; 8. ?; 9. !; 10. ?; 11. !; 12. !

Page 85

1. Spring Grove, Minnesota; 2. Dear Gramps,; 3. Your cousin,; 4. October 9, 2001; 5. North Branch, New York; 6. Dear Uncle Gerald,; 7. March 3, 2001; 8. Fall Leaf, KS: Letter: Ocean View, California; October 15, 2001; Dear Josie and Ted,; Reno, Nevada,; Barstow, California,; Your friend,

Page 86

1. no; 2. no; 3. yes; 4. no; 5. yes; 6. Debbie, Don, and Dan were impressed with New York City.; 7. It is an important business, culture, and trade center.; 8. The Bronx, Manhattan, Queens, Brooklyn, and Staten Island are its five boroughs.; 9. Chinatown, Greenwich Village, and Harlem are three neighborhoods in Manhattan.; 10. The Smith's saw Times Square, Rockefeller Center, and the United Nations Headquarters.; 11. Central Park surprised them with its grass, trees, lakes, and hills in the heart of the city.; 12. New York City has many concert halls, theaters, and museums.; 13. The Smith's visited the Metropolitan Museum of Art, the Guggenheim Museum, and the American Museum of Natural History.

Page 87

1. Kim, let's look at this book about falcons.; 2. Falcons, like hawks, have hooked beaks and feet with claws.; 3. Falcons are powerful fliers, and they can swoop from great heights.; 4. The American kestrel, the smallest North American falcon, is only 8 inches long.; 5. A bird of prey, the American kestrel, eats insects, mice, lizards, and other birds.; 6. Peregrine falcons, amazing flyers, can reach speeds of 200 miles per hour. 7. What do peregrines prefer to eat, Alex?; 8. They eat birds, and that is why they are sometimes called duck hawks.; 9. The gyrfalcon, the largest species of falcon, is 2 feet long.; 10. Gyrfalcons live in Arctic regions, Kim.

Answer Key

Page 88

1. Cassie said, "Nadia was a marvelous gymnast from Romania."; 2. "She won everyone's heart in 1976," continued Cassie.; 3. Cory asked, "What happened to make Nadia so popular?"; 4. Cassie said, "First she won the American Cup Championship."; 5. "She scored a perfect 10 for her vault," Cassie explained.; 6. Cassie added, "Then Nadia received a 10 for her floor exercise."; 7. Cory asked, "Did she ever perform in the Olympics?"; 8. "Yes, she won three gold medals, a silver medal, and a bronze medal in 1976."

Page 89

1. "Master of All Masters"; 2. "The Golden Touch"; 3. "Hidden Hunter"; 4. "Scuba, Anyone?"; 5. "Stop the Food Fight!"; 6. "Spin Control"; 7. "Leader of the Pack"; 8. "Monster Mash"; 9. "Y.M.C.A."; 10. "Castle on a Cloud"; 11. "Hear America Singing"; 12. "Cat and the Weather"; 13. "A Modern Dragon"; 14. "Paul Revere's Ride"

Page 90

1. you've; 2. we're; 3. he'll; 4. haven't; 5. she's; 6. I'm; 7. Rudyard Kipling's stories; 8. Hans Christian Andersen's tales; 9. David Small's illustrations; 10. PN; 11. C; 12. PN; 13. C; 14. PN; 15. C

Unit 6 Test

1. A; 2. B; 3. B; 4. D; 5. C; 6. D; 7. C; 8. C; 9. D; 10. B; 11. D; 12. A; 13. C; 14. C; 15. D; 16. C; 17. B; 18. C; 19. B; 20. C; Constructed response: In the first sentence, three girls order pizza. Four girls order pizza in the second sentence.; Answers will vary.

Page 96

1. chews; 2. cheap; 3. alter; 4. bail; 5. bore; 6. manor; 7. raze; 8. tiers; 9. poll; 10. lesson; 11. meet, meat; 12. stares, stairs; 13. might, mite; 14. peers, piers

Page 97

1. aids; 2. or; 3. They're; 4. use; 5. for; 6. board; 7. tow; 8. sea; 9. lone; 10. scene; 11. time; 12. way

Page 98

1. It; 2. They; 3. them; 4. It; 5. It; 6. He; 7. We; 8. them

Page 99

1. forgave, forgiven; 2. lost, lost; 3. told, told; 4. rang, rung; 5. sewed, sewn; 6. gave, given; 7. read; 8. grew; 9. began; 10. held; 11. won; 12. led; 13. was; 14. made; 15. left; 16. came

Page 100

1. kept; 2. made; 3. thought; 4. knew; 5. drew; 6. saw; 7. felt; 8. became; 9. built; 10. led; 1.–2. Sentences will vary.

Page 101

1. cover; 2. contain; 3. live; 4. affect; 5. comes; 6. damages; 7. pollute; 8. carry; 9. kill; 10. dump; 11. creates; 12. drown; 13. decays; 14. prohibits

Page 102

1. grow; 2. vary; 3. reaches; 4. look; 5. help; 6. holds; 7. keeps; 8. absorb; 9. protect; 10. grow; 11. occur

Page 103

1. Jim, Sean, and Maria liked to visit Grandma and Grandpa.; 2. Grandpa had horses, cows, and pigs on his farm.; 3. Grandma raised chickens, ducks, and geese.; 4. Daisies, tulips, and roses grew in her garden.; 5. Jim and Sean planted tomatoes, green peppers, and carrots in the garden.; 6. Maria grew beautiful daffodils, snapdragons, and marigolds.

Page 104

1. Rob studied his notes, organized them, and wrote an outline.; 2. Rob wrote a rough draft, revised it, and proofread it.; 3. Rob made corrections, copied the report, and shared it with the class.; 4. Rob reported about Yosemite National Park, showed pictures of the park, and gave its history.; 5. The students listened carefully, asked questions, and learned about Yosemite National Park.; 6. Rob smiled, thanked the class for their attention, and returned to his seat.

Page 105

1. The trail was narrow and rocky.; 2. The trail zig-zagged steeply and sharply to the left.; 3. Rita nervously and intently watched the edge of the trail.; 4. The trail suddenly and abruptly ended at the dock.; 5. We saw a breathtaking and spectacular sight.; 6. Crater Lake is a sapphire-blue color and extremely clear.

Page 106

1. juicy; 2. two; 3. small; 4. pale; 5. underground; 6. warm; 7. well-drained; 8. deeply; 9. well; 10. four; 11. carefully; 12. now; 13. twenty

Page 107

1. apples; 2. carrots; 3. milk; 4. cookies; 5. cashier; 6. groceries; 7. rode; 8. played; 9. chased; 10. jogged; 11. scampered; 12. dived

Page 108

1. fabulous; 2. ornately; 3. eagerly; 4. thirty-year-old; 5. huge; 6. absolutely; 7. magnificently; 8. brilliantly; 9. enthusiastically; 10. splendid; 11. delicate; 12. difficult; 13. beautifully; 14. world-famous; 15. joyously

Page 109

1. better; 2. best; 3. good; 4. bad; 5. worse; 6. worst; 7. good; 8. best; 9. bad; 10. good

Page 110

1. well; 2. well; 3. badly; 4. better; 5. better; 6. worse; 7. well; 8. worse; 9. best; 10. better

Page 111

1. There aren't flamingos living anywhere by me.; 2. Can't anybody tell me where they live?; 3. There aren't any other wading birds as big and colorful.; 4. I don't know of any birds besides flamingos that eat upside-down.; 5. I wouldn't ever think it possible for a bird to eat so much algae.; 6. I never saw any other birds stand on one leg like flamingos.; 7. There must not be anything else like flamingos.

Unit 7 Test

1. C; 2. B; 3. C; 4. C; 5. D; 6. B; 7. C; 8. A; 9. C; 10. A; 11. B; 12. D; 13. A; 14. C; 15. A; 16. D; 17. C; 18. C; 19. A; 20. C; Constructed response: two negatives; Answers will vary.

Final Review Test

1. B; 2. H; 3. B; 4. J; 5. C; 6. F; 7. B; 8. J; 9. B; 10. H; 11. A; 12. H; 13. A; 14. J; 15. B; 16. G; 17. C; 18. G; 19. C; 20. G; 21. C; 22. G; 23. D; 24. J; 25. A; 26. H; 27. D; 28. J; 29. C; 30. J; Constructed-response answers will vary.